EXTRAVAGANT
Grace

WOMEN OF FAITH™

EXTRAVAGANT
Grace

Devotions That Celebrate God's Gift of Grace

Patsy Clairmont

Barbara Johnson

Marilyn Meberg

Luci Swindoll

Sheila Walsh

Thelma Wells

Traci Mullins, General Editor

ZONDERVAN™

GRAND RAPIDS, MICHIGAN 49530 USA

ZONDERVAN™

Extravagant Grace
Copyright © 2000 by Women of Faith, Inc.

Requests for information should be addressed to:

Zondervan, *Grand Rapids, Michigan 49530*

ISBN 0-310-25436-1

All Scripture quotations, unless otherwise indicated, are taken from the *Holy Bible: New International Version*®. NIV®. Copyright © 1973, 1978, 1984 by International Bible Society. Used by permission of Zondervan. All rights reserved.

Other Scripture quotations are from:

New American Standard Bible (NASB), © 1960, 1977 by the Lockman Foundation;

The Message, © 1993, 1994, 1995 by Eugene H. Peterson;

The Living Bible (TLB), © 1971 by Tyndale House Publishers;

New King James Version (NKJV), © 1982 by Thomas Nelson, Inc.;

Revised Standard Version (RSV), © 1965 by Zondervan;

King James Version (KJV).

All rights reserved. No part of this publication may be reproduced, stored in a retrieval system, or transmitted in any form or by any means—electronic, mechanical, photocopy, recording, or any other—except for brief quotations in printed reviews, without the prior permission of the publisher.

Published in association with the literary agency of Alive Communications, Inc., 7680 Goddard Street, Suite 200, Colorado Springs, CO 80920.

Interior design by Amy E. Langeler

Printed in the United States of America

03 04 05 06 07 08 09 /❖ OP/ 10 9 8 7 6 5 4 3 2 1

Contents

-ENJOYING THE GIFT-

-SHARING THE GIFT-

-CELEBRATING THE GIFT-

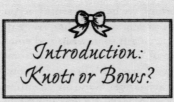

Introduction: Knots or Bows?

PATSY CLAIRMONT

❧

When the enormous box arrived on my doorstep last April, I couldn't imagine what was inside. I figured that, since it was my birthday, a friend had remembered me in some thoughtful way. But the container's size confounded me.

Being unrestrainedly enthusiastic about gifts, I could hardly wait to untie the ribbon, tear off the wrappings, and discover my surprise. I barely had the package in the door before I started to rip with zeal. Then I began to giggle, for I discovered a party was in the box, replete with hats, horns, and confetti. What fun! Also tucked into the package was a trove of individually wrapped presents with my name artistically printed on each gift tag. Yes-s-s!

Extravagant Grace is not a party in a box, but a party in a book. We would like each reading to be a gift for you, designed with your day in mind. And not just on your birthday, but on a trove of other days that we girls — Sheila, Patsy, Thelma, Barbara, Marilyn, and Luci — want to help you celebrate. We're wearing the hats and trumpeting the horns in your honor.

Most important, we have presents for you. Each chapter is a present to remind you that every day you draw breath is a gift . . . a gift to unwrap and enjoy.

My Women of Faith teammates are some of the most dynamic gift givers around. These gals know how to enter a day with extravagance! Why, on Valentine's Day I saw Luci sporting a set of large red wax lips while Thelma was hugging a huge stuffed bumblebee . . . so I know we're going to laugh at this party. The Queen of Fun, Barbara, will keep us chortling for sure.

Collectively we are about the age of England. Or is it the Great Wall of China? Only kidding . . . but between us we do have decades of experience unwrapping many a day. Some of those days were thrilling, some mundane, and others devastating. So we've decided to give you something that has helped us through the unfolding of our lives — the gift of grace.

Well, actually, we aren't the Grace Giver, but we know the Extravagant One who is. What we offer is our understanding of grace as we've embraced this gift for ourselves.

Speaking of gifts, recently I was given a tea basket that included — what else — a box of tea. On the box was a statement accompanied by a question. The statement was, "Life is a ribbon." I like that gifty thought. The question was, "What are you tying, knots or bows?" Hmm, now that's convicting. After all, we each have knotted days that don't feel like gifts, and we all experience days in which we're decked out in bows.

Now, I have to confess that the thought of us covered in bows makes me giggle because Marilyn and Sheila don't do frilly; they're definitely tailored. I've seen them turn shades of lime green when things became too cutesy. But I'm your layered-lace girl with twirling ribbons spewing in all directions.

That's one of the things we've loved about doing this purposeful party together: we've all brought our unique ways to the festivities. And, more important, we've brought his unfailing ways.

Please join the party. C'mon, sport a zany hat, honk your horn, and toss confetti all over your life. We have reason to rejoice! Together with God's help we'll unravel knots and create exquisite bows as we learn to gift wrap our days in his extravagant grace.

Just imagine that each chapter is a gift for you, with *your* name on the gift tag. Yes-s-s!

The Gift

Pictures of Grace

PATSY CLAIRMONT

We bring nothing to God, and He gives us everything.
GARY THOMAS

What picture comes to mind when you hear the word *grace?* I think of a woman named — what else — Grace who lived near our family's home when I was growing up. She and her husband were friends of my parents and, believe me, that's where the friendship ended. Grace had no, uh, grace for children. She and her husband didn't have little ones of their own so perhaps that's why Grace had no space in her heart for me.

Of course, I was a precocious pip-squeak, quite full of myself. I was a second child, the first girl, who arrived in our family after a nine-year interval. That gave me some distinct advantages, of which I took full advantage. Grace evidently struggled with my indulged ways. I, too, struggled . . . with Grace.

Years later, in desperate hours of my life, I experienced another grace: God's grace. The Lord gave me a place to stand in his presence — me, the precocious kid, now a confused adult. I couldn't believe he had space in his heart for me. This undeserved reception and inclusion stunned me. And, honestly, I struggled . . . with grace.

Two distinct pictures of "grace." One portrays not even a smidgen of favor or friendly regard; the other speaks of lavish acceptance. I had trouble with both.

I couldn't bear the feelings I had when I was in Grace's home. I felt physically rigid and certain that if I bumped anything or dropped something my life expectancy would be reduced drastically. Yet what troubled me most wasn't just the sense that I might do something wrong but the feeling I *was* something wrong.

God's grace, which gave me the freedom to be myself without condemnation, was not only foreign but also a little frightening. I was used to trying to win approval and not receiving it until I had performed some necessary stunts, like making my bed, saying my prayers, and attending church thirty-three times a week. Unmerited favor is hard to swallow, and yet, when received, it sweetly quenches my deep thirst for unconditional love.

A third picture of grace comes to my mind — the grace depicted in a painting of an iris. Actually two paintings: one portrays beds of this lovely, elegant flower; the other a single iris. When you view these famous works of art, you see only the flowers; you have no sense of their location. Are they in a city park, a flowered field, or perhaps on a rambling farm?

There's a reason for the mystery. Not only does the artist's selective focus keep us from being distracted by peripheral objects, we also aren't alerted to the artist's real world. The painter, Vincent van Gogh, created his masterpieces in an asylum.

In some of the darkest hours of his life, van Gogh found a single, graceful flower, and he made that his focus. His outside world at the asylum was grim at best, and everything around him was a reminder of his internal sadness. Yet somehow van Gogh, when he saw the irises, was able to connect himself to the only lovely thing in his surroundings. Captured by the flowers' gracefulness, he painted them several times. Yet it is believed he never found the inner grace or peace he was searching for. He never saw beyond the purple iris to its providential Designer. He struggled ... with grace.

I, too, have seen grace in God's creations — a swan gliding across a still pond, a gazelle leaping across an African plain, an eagle soaring above a craggy cliff. As effortless as those movements are, so is the ease with which God bestows his extravagant gift of grace into our lives.

Grace is stunning. It is breathtaking. It is more beautiful than van Gogh's *Irises*. Grace finds us in our poverty and presents us with the gift of an inheritance we didn't deserve ... the gift of grace.

Grace to you and peace from God our Father
and the Lord Jesus Christ.

PHILEMON 1:3

🌿

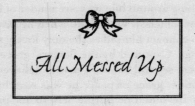

All Messed Up

THELMA WELLS

&

It is only God that may be had for the asking.

LOWELL

*O*nce upon a time, almighty God looked upon an unformed mass and said, "I'm going to make a world."

So he made the birds and the bees, the flowers and the trees, the stars up above . . . and a thing called LOVE! And that was good!

Then, when he wanted someone who could speak the language of his heart and have sweet fellowship with him, he made a man and a woman. But they became arrogant and wanted to be as smart as God, so they disobeyed his simple instructions for how to live happily ever after. They messed up. So God threw them out of their magnificent Garden home.

God's first people bore a lot of children, but they were all disobedient just like their parents. They messed up. So God did away with them all, except his servant Noah, Noah's family, and a menagerie of birds and beasts.

At first Noah was very grateful for God's favor. Noah followed God's instructions to the letter and built an ark.

Noah was doubly grateful when his ark sailed through the deadly flood God sent to destroy everything on the earth. But when the rains stopped, Noah got drunk and messed up with God.

God then thought, "I know someone I can trust to be the father of many nations. Maybe he'll understand how much I love him, and perhaps he'll do the right thing."

So God chose Abraham as his own. But Abe got impatient, had a baby by a woman other than his wife, and messed up with God. God still loved him though, and in his grace he finally gave Abraham the son he'd promised.

Abraham's son Isaac wasn't perfect either. Neither was Isaac's son Jacob. One by one they kept messing up with God.

So God anointed priests. They messed up. He gave authority to judges. They messed up. He sent the prophets. They all messed up.

I can just hear God saying, "If you want something done right, you've got to do it yourself." So God put on the skin of a man and came to earth to live, love, and die so that every messy person could have perfect fellowship with him.

That's called grace incarnate. When God sent his son, Jesus, to live among us and die for our sins, he knew we did not and never would deserve this kind of sacrificial love. But he also knew we would continue to mess up until the end of time. We could never save ourselves, so he poured out his life for us and brought us back into the Garden of his love.

What a gift! Knowing that God's Son died a cruel death on an old rugged cross so that I can have an intimate relationship with the Almighty makes me want to reach out my short, chubby arms, grab Jesus around his neck, and hug him the way my grandchildren hug me tight and say, "Grammy, I love you!" Even when they've misbehaved, they can come to me and steal my heart with their sweet embrace.

When we embrace the grace of God, we can come to him with the spirit of a little child and say, "Father, I've messed up. Please forgive me. I love you!" Instantly, faster than a grandmother's pardon, God grants us his unmerited favor through Christ Jesus and loves us freely once more.

What a gift! When you mess up, God's there to clean you up. Just run to him with your arms open wide. He'll return your embrace every time.

> *The LORD, the LORD, the compassionate and*
> *gracious God, slow to anger, abounding in love*
> *and faithfulness, maintaining love to thousands,*
> *and forgiving wickedness, rebellion and sin.*
>
> EXODUS 34:6–7

~

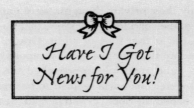

Have I Got News for You!

SHEILA WALSH

❧

Salvation is a gift and you can't boast about a gift.
You can only be thankful.

D. JAMES KENNEDY

*I*t had been a long day for Grace. She finished her shift
at the dollar store at five o'clock and hurried home to
fix a meal for her husband, Stan, and their four boys.
What can we have that's quick? she thought, as she stood in
line waiting for the number ten bus. Her back ached from
being on her feet all day, and the thought of going out
again at 11:30 that night sent a throb deeper into her
weary bones. Since Stan's accident the previous year, she
had become the sole breadwinner and taken on job number two: cleaning at the local hospital three nights a week.

Grace arrived for her shift at one minute before midnight to join her two coworkers as they filled up their
buckets with steaming hot water and shuffled down the
corridor to begin the long night's scrub-down. All three
women had a lot on their minds. Mary was worried about
her daughter's grades. Stella hoped that no one noticed
how often she slipped into the restroom to take a quick
swig from the flask in her pocket.

Suddenly their private thoughts were punctuated by a noise down the corridor. They knew that no one should be in that area at that time of night. Grace, Mary, and Stella picked up their mops — poor weapons against any real threat — and stealthily approached the door from where the mysterious noise seemed to be coming. Warily, Grace opened the door . . . and beheld the most beautiful sight she had ever seen in her long, hard life. Filling the room with the wingspan of a thousand eagles stood an angel, a messenger from God, with this outrageous message:

"Grace! Have I got news for you! God is here! To you, Grace, with your varicose veins, your PMS, your two-pack-a-day habit . . . to you is born a Savior. Today. The love of God has come to you, Stella, and to you, Mary. God is with you."

This fable illustrates the simple, joyful message of the Gospel — just as it was presented on the first Christmas. After four hundred years of silence following the close of the Old Testament, God showed up on the night shift, to the shepherds. In the voice of his archangel he proclaimed salvation to the boys on the hill.

This radical gift of grace shows us that God's love is based on nothing we have done, but on who he is. Do you think God looked down at a few shepherds under the stars and thought, "These are the only guys who have their act together. I think I'll break the news to them first." I don't think so. God so longed for us to get the message of grace that he chose to display his glory to people like you and me who try so hard and fail so often. He shows up to people who slip into the bathroom for a quick shot of something to deaden the pain of life. He shows up to all the broken, lonely people of the world with the Good News: God is here!

It's hard to grasp that truth, living in this culture of ours where we worship at the altar of apparent success. We think that God will show up for the Billy Grahams, the Joyce Meyerses, the Women of Faith of this world . . . but not for us. It's as if we think that certain people have a hot line to heaven, a special number that God answers before he bothers with the regular office line.

It's time to go back to the Word of God and ask for eyes to see and ears to hear the way things really are. Christ came to the factory workers of his day. He was born on the wrong side of the tracks. He chose a fourteen-year-old virgin to be his mother. He was a blue-collar worker — he did manual labor all his adult life. His friends were a mixed bunch, and he was criticized for that. But grace won the day.

"While Jesus was having dinner at Matthew's house, many tax collectors and 'sinners' came and ate with him and his disciples. When the Pharisees saw this, they asked his disciples, 'Why does your teacher eat with tax collectors and "sinners"?' On hearing this, Jesus said, 'It is not the healthy who need a doctor, but the sick. But go and learn what this means: "I desire mercy, not sacrifice." For I have not come to call the righteous, but sinners'" (Matthew 9:10–13).

That's the gift! The gift of grace is given to those of us who think we are worthy — until Christ in his mercy shows us we are not. The gift of grace is given to those of us who know we are not worthy — and yet Christ meets us in dark places, in hospital corridors, with cigarettes hanging out of our mouths and fear on our faces. He came to Grace, to Mary, to Stella . . . to you and to me. What a gift! All we can do is kneel down and worship . . . and be thankful.

For it is by grace you have been saved,
through faith—and this not from yourselves,
it is the gift of God.

EPHESIANS 2:8

One-Way Street

LUCI SWINDOLL

❧

*I believe that God did lean down to become Man
in order that we could reach up to Him.*

MALCOLM MUGGERIDGE

I love words. Words, and their meanings, are fascinating to me. When Malcolm Muggeridge says, "God did lean down to become Man," I am struck by the power of his words. They convey the incredible thought that deity and humanity are one, in Christ. A profound truth, simply stated.

There's also something fun about playing with words. If you've seen the "Sniglets" calendar, you know what I mean. For example, in "Sniglets," *profanitype* is a word that means "special symbols used by cartoonists to replace swear words." Or, how about *umbroglio* — "any conflict with an umbrella on a windy day." I also like *Jemimites*. These are extremely tiny pancakes formed from the batter that falls off the ladle.

Some of my favorite authors are those who do original gymnastics with words or phrases. The witty and erudite Dorothy Parker was once asked to make a sentence with the word "horticulture." In a flash she shot back, "You can lead a horticulture but you can't make her think." Or how about Molly Ivins, a journalist from Texas. She coined the word "fize"... as in, "Fize younger I'd move to Europe" or, "Fize a rich woman I'd drive a better car."

I've been known to conveniently create a few words (or definitions of words) myself when the ones I had just wouldn't do. I remember one summer making a big sign for a Fourth of July party at Marilyn's house. Her daughter Beth and I worked on it for days. It was red, white, and blue, of course, and it stretched across the entire backyard. In big block letters we spelled out, LETH TAKE JULY BY FOURTH.

Then there was the Christmas when I wanted to make a card for my dear friend Mary Graham to commemorate the season in a unique and special way. She had just returned from a mission trip to Russia, so I drew a Russian Orthodox church, complete with cupolas, on the front of the card. Under it I planned to write "Merry Christmas" in Russian. But when I searched my books, the library, dictionaries, etc., I could not find out how to say "Merry Christmas" in that language.

When my quest proved fruitless, I didn't give up. I simply found a short Russian word followed by a long one (looked like Merry Christmas to me!) and used them. Mary didn't read Russian, so she'd never know. The words I chose actually meant "One-Way Street." As I printed them under the church in Cyrillic script, it hit me: "One-Way Street" was a very appropriate way to say Merry Christmas! So, I added this note to the card:

"Actually, I wanted this to say Merry Christmas in Russian, but I couldn't find it. So it says One-Way Street,

which is sort of the same thing when you think about it.
The birth of Christ is the One Way to peace, hope, joy,
laughter . . . all that Christmas means. May Christmas be
all of that and more to you, dearest Mary — a one-way
street to happiness."

We've had so much fun with that card. And on blus-
tery December days we smile at total strangers and say
with a big grin, "One-Way Street!"

"For God so loved the world that he gave his one and
only Son, that whoever believes in him shall not perish
but have eternal life" (John 3:16). You couldn't make up
better words than those! They are your one-way street to
life. A gift for all eternity.

Fize you, I'd believe it.

> *Jesus answered, "I am the way and the truth*
> *and the life. No one comes to the*
> *Father except through me."*
>
> JOHN 14:6

✌

Grace Period

THELMA WELLS

❧

Our failure is frightful, our falling inglorious,
our dying wretched. Yet never does love's compassionate eye
turn from us, nor the operation of mercy cease.

JULIAN OF NORWICH

My husband, George, and I were blessed with financial comfort from the day we married, April Fools' Day 1961, until the year 1986. During that time, we never had a bill collector call us or have threats flood our mailbox. We were always able to buy much of what we wanted. When our children were small, I was a stay-at-home mom. When they started kindergarten, I went back to work, not because I had to but because I wanted to. I was a bank officer at the largest independent bank in Texas, where I had clout, prestige, notoriety, authority, insurance, and a paycheck. Thangs were purty.

In 1980, I decided to go into the speaking business for myself. Teaching for the American Institute of Banking had opened the door for me to be a frequent speaker for financial institutions across the country. My business was firmly established by 1984 when I resigned from the bank to be a full-time entrepreneur. My calendar was full with speaking engagements and long-term training contracts. Money was no object because I was making plenty of it — until 1986!

You know what happened. Banks started failing and falling like flies. Within six weeks after the worm turned, I lost all my speaking contracts as Texas banks tumbled.

Outside banking I had no credibility, but not being one of faint heart, I thought I was good enough to market myself fast enough to be on my feet in short order. Not! For one year, I cold-called, beat the pavement, mailed brochures, joined networking organizations, wrote a column for a neighborhood newspaper, socialized, fraternized, and did everything in my power to get work. Nothing worked!

By now, money was running out. I had overextended myself during the good times and run up the balances on my credit cards. I now was on a first-name basis with several bill collectors.

Even though I had written to all my creditors and explained our situation, it didn't help when I had to take their calls. So I took advantage of my situation and their time to present Jesus in some way. When a collector called, I would ask if he or she had ever been in my situation. Sometimes my question would spark conversation. Other times the collector would become hostile and rude. In either case, I'd listen, then give what I thought would be a friendly and appropriate response. I actually started to count it a blessing from God that my unpleasant financial situation gave me the opportunity to talk to these people. I had a working telephone that could be used to help bring people into the kingdom!

During that period of financial drought, God led three of those creditors to extend grace to me. Two allowed my good credit rating to stand while I continued to make small monthly payments. One creditor just stopped sending bills. Thirteen years ago, they just stopped coming! I've heard of a grace period for paying bills, but I'd never heard of a grace decade for a debt owed. That creditor exonerated me. All my creditors were lenient. Oh, what grace!

I did not deserve the goodness I received. It was granted, though, in spite of me. Good times returned. There were new contracts. Cash flowed again. I paid my bills and began to get on my feet again. Everything I thought I had lost during that down time has been regained, and more.

My creditors gave me favor, mercy, forgiveness, compassion, tolerance, and pardon. My debts were finally paid. In full.

And my creditors' grace is only a flicker of the splendor of God's grace toward each of us. When you and I overextended ourselves in sin and owed a debt we could not pay, Jesus paid it in full on the cross of Calvary by shedding his blood, dying, and rising again. Through his blood, we are granted complete pardon and total salvation. We did nothing to deserve it. Because he wanted an intimate relationship with us that could not exist until our debt was paid, our Father sent his only Son to pay off our account. In full.

Marvelous, infinite, matchless grace! It's yours, my friend. Receive it.

For Christ died for sins once for all, the righteous
for the unrighteous, to bring you to God.

1 PETER 3:18

❧

Princess Fur-Face

MARILYN MEBERG

❧

*I do not at all understand the mystery of grace—only that he
meets us where we are but does not leave us where he found us.*

ANNE LAMOTT

"Whad'ya say we change the furniture around?" Ken
queried one Saturday morning as we were finish-
ing our last cups of coffee/tea. "Let's put the couch by the
window and the two chairs facing the fireplace." I had
learned years before to trust Ken's fine eye for furniture
placement.

"Sounds good to me, Babe," I said, "but do you have
the stamina for Ashley's neurotic response?"

Ashley was our cocker spaniel who reacted strongly
against all visual changes. She wanted things to remain in
their accustomed spots. If they didn't, she had one of her
"spells." It didn't matter how big or small the change; each
warranted a protest. Let me give you an example.

A friend popped in on me one morning and for some
reason just dropped her purse in the middle of the floor
as we made our way to the "chat chairs" by the window.
(This was before the rearrangement.) Several moments
later Ashley, who hated to miss anything, came trotting

33

into the room. Spotting my friend's purse in the middle of the floor, she skidded to a stiff-legged halt, stared briefly at the purse, and went into a dramatic fit of barking. Slowly circling the purse, she barked, growled, and scowled until my friend finally placed her purse behind the chair. Gradually Ashley settled down, but it was obvious the visit was ruined for her.

As Ken pondered the price to be paid for furniture rearrangement, he noted that Ashley was out on the deck dozing in the sun. She might not notice what was going on until the dastardly deed was done.

Several hours later Ashley roused herself from her siesta and ambled into the house. She immediately assessed that unauthorized changes had occurred in her absence. After barking herself nearly hoarse, she flounced out of the living room and stayed in her "sleep area" for several days. We delivered her food and water. Gradually she came to realize that the couch was now in a far better spot for her because she was able to see out the window. (Of course she was allowed on the furniture!) This made it possible for her to visually patrol the neighborhood without leaving the comforts of home.

Perhaps the greatest trauma Princess Fur-Face had to endure was when we got a new car. Ashley's sleep area was in a small room adjoining the garage, and although the car wasn't fully visible to her, it was in close proximity.

On the first night of their cohabitation, Ashley, who had not yet been introduced to the new car, scampered down the stairs to bed as was her custom. We stood behind the closed door holding our breath. No sound . . . no barking . . . no response at all. Ken's theory was that because it was dark, Ashley couldn't see the car. Our intention was to later, in the daylight, gradually coax her into an accepting relationship with the new vehicle.

Around 1 A.M. we were awakened by the sound of frantic, ferocious barking. Ashley had discovered the car. Fearing she'd disturb the neighbors, Ken flew down the stairs, scooped up Ashley along with her bed, and deposited her in our room, something Ken normally refused to do. She grumbled and complained the rest of the night, but at least she didn't bark.

Because Ken drove the car to work during the day, I had no opportunity to ease Ashley into a spirit of charitableness about the car. Each night she seemed to forget about the alien in the garage when she first went to bed, then rediscover it sometime after midnight.

At 2 A.M. on the fourth night of Ashley's histrionics, Ken exasperatedly dragged himself out of bed and announced he had just come up with a plan which required that we both get dressed and take Ashley for a ride.

"Are you going to dump her out of the car somewhere in another county?" I asked cautiously as I threw on jeans and a sweatshirt.

"Trust me" was all he said.

Ken thrust a squirming, growling, barking cocker into my arms, and we got in the monster car to begin what Ken said would be the "taming ride." For at least an hour Ashley was a bundle of growling rigidity in my arms. With the radio playing soft music and both of us stroking Ashley with words of love and encouragement (none of which we felt at that moment), Ashley began to relax. An hour and a half later and miles from home, she went limp in my arms and fell asleep. From that moment on, Ashley had peace about her metal roommate. In fact, one of her favorite activities became riding in that car.

I hate to tell you how closely I identify with Ashley at times. There are God-gifts I have fought so fervently only to find that once I yield my resisting spirit I reap incredible benefits. For example, I certainly don't overtly resist the concept of grace, but I've tried to earn it a million times. I seem to tenaciously cling to the mistaken notion that I've got to be good enough in order to deserve grace. How many times does God have to hold my rigidly resisting spirit until finally, with celestial music in my ears, I relax and embrace his gift?

Ashley learned with just one ride.

> *No eye has seen, no ear has heard,*
> *no mind has conceived what God has*
> *prepared for those who love him.*
>
> 1 CORINTHIANS 2:9

  ❧

"I Took Your Place"

SHEILA WALSH

᷾

God does not give grace freely in the sense that He will demand no satisfaction, but He gave Christ to be the satisfaction for us.

MARTIN LUTHER

My mother never ceases to amaze me. She is defi-nitely a pioneer at heart. When Barry and I lived in Laguna Beach, California, she came to visit. Since she can't drive, she was at the mercy of my schedule — or so I thought. But one day I caught her busily preparing to head out of the door on some adventure of her own.

"Where are you going, Mum?" I asked.

"To San Juan, Capistrano," she replied with an excited grin.

"How are you going to get there?"

"The bus."

"We have buses here?"

"Of course you do," she said.

"How do you know?"

"Oh, I made inquiries."

"How did you know where to inquire?" I pressed.

"I just know these things," she said with a smile. And she was gone. I'd lived in Laguna for a year and had no clue that there was a bus, never mind one to the old Spanish mission.

Mum always jumps headfirst into life, but even I wasn't prepared for her comment on the phone one day after she'd returned to Scotland. "Well, that's my first school mission over," she said.

"This is a bad line, Mum," I replied. "I thought you said you'd just finished your first school mission."

"I did," she answered. "Your phone's fine."

Well, I was more than curious and asked for details. Apparently one of the local schools in my hometown of Ayr wanted someone to come to speak to the students about faith. Not realizing that I was now living in America, the principal called my mum's number to get in touch with me. She explained that I was in the U.S. but volunteered to come in my place.

You could have knocked me over with a feather. You see, my mum is nothing like me. She is a quiet, gentle, behind-the-scenes kind of person.

"What on earth possessed you to volunteer?" I asked incredulously.

"Well, I saw it as an opportunity to share the Gospel with these young people, and I didn't want it to go to waste."

That shut me up. I was so proud of her.

"So how did it go?" I asked.

"God was very faithful," she replied, "and I was very nervous. But it went well. I knew if you had been here you would have gone, so I took your place."

Yeah, Mum!

My mother's "boldly going where no Scottish mother has gone before" exploit is a small picture of the great truth of the Gospel. While you and I were unavailable and unable to atone for our own sins, Christ took our place.

Now that's extravagant grace! So when you feel unworthy, when you've blown it again, remember the bottom-line truth of your life: Christ took your place, was punished for your sins, and now stands ever before you with his arms full of a bouquet of grace — just for you.

> *But we see Jesus, who was made a little lower*
> *than the angels, now crowned with glory and*
> *honor because he suffered death, so that by the*
> *grace of God he might taste death for everyone.*
>
> HEBREWS 2:9

🙟

No More Performances

MARILYN MEBERG

ર૭

Most Christians live their lives as though they're going to be graded once a year by a God who stands there frowning with his hands stuck in the pockets of his robe.

CHUCK SWINDOLL

*H*ave you ever stayed up past midnight to make heart-shaped sugar cookies for your third grader's Valentine's Day party, only to watch your little ningnong grab your carefully arranged creations the next morning and dash out the door without even saying "Thanks, Mom"?

Have you ever put in several hours of overtime on the job helping to train your new replacement ... you know, the one who couldn't be more than eleven years old and still can't read or count past six? Did anyone bother to say how much your efforts were appreciated?

We live in a world where we expect to be appreciated; we want a reward for a good performance. We also live in a world where we expect criticism for a bad performance. Unfortunately, we're all familiar with words like these: "Mom, those cookies were rock hard. Bobby lost a tooth." Or "Thank goodness we've finally got someone on the job who can type!" Rewards and punishments. It's the way the system works, and we're used to it.

And yet Jesus, when he was here, turned that familiar system upside down. Instead of emphasizing the value of performance, he affirmed the value of the person.

For example, when Jesus met the Samaritan woman at the well (John 4), he already knew she had a colorful past. In fact, he shocked her by telling her about her five husbands as well as the man with whom she was living who didn't happen to be her spouse. But in spite of her history, he looked beyond her performance and zeroed in on her person. Knowing her insatiable thirst for a meaningful relationship, he offered her living water which, were she to drink it, would quench her thirst for eternity.

When Jesus was passing through Jericho (Luke 19), a short little guy named Zacchaeus ingeniously climbed a tree so that he could see Jesus. As Jesus was passing by, he stopped, looked up into the tree, and called out to the little man: "Zacchaeus, come down immediately. I must stay at your house today" (Luke 19:5). Zacchaeus was stunned; the people were furious. This guy was as crooked as a dog's hind leg. As a tax collector he overcharged his own people, pocketed the surplus, and gave the remaining amount to the corrupt Roman government. Zacchaeus was one despised citizen. But Jesus cut through his disgusting performance to the hidden person Jesus wanted to love into the kingdom of God.

We see the same upside-down system in operation when a woman, caught in the act of adultery, is brought into the presence of Jesus as one who should be stoned to death according to Jewish law. You will remember Jesus was silent for a period of time and then spoke these now familiar words: "If any one of you is without sin, let him be the first to throw a stone at her" (John 8:7). When everyone ultimately slipped away, Jesus simply said to the woman, "Go now and leave your life of sin" (John 8:11). He looked beyond her performance to see the person who, in her poverty of soul and overwhelming shame, needed his compassion.

Jesus further confounded his listeners by telling them the story of two brothers, one of whom followed the rules and the other who broke them all (Luke 15). The point of the parable is that the father loved each of his boys to the same degree. When the prodigal who performed so badly returned home, he was embraced by the father and even given a homecoming party. The son who had always done everything right was not loved more; his performance did not increase the father's love any more than the other son's lack of performance decreased the father's love.

This message was incomprehensible to the people of Jesus' day. Not only was their social system maintained by performance, so was their religious system. They had a system of do's and don'ts which left no doubt about how they were to conduct their lives. They couldn't figure out what Jesus was talking about! Whatever it was, it totally unsettled their system and made them either angry or confused.

The Pharisees were furious when Jesus pointed out that very moral deficiency. He said to them, "You have heard that it was said, 'Do not commit adultery.' But I tell you that anyone who looks at a woman lustfully has already committed adultery with her in his heart" (Matthew 5:27–28).

If that's the case, how, then, is anyone good enough for God? That's the whole point. No one is! Because if our behavior doesn't condemn us, then our thought life does. God knows that, looks beyond our imperfect performance, and loves and receives us anyway. Jesus made that kind of grace possible on the cross by dying for the sin that inspires bad performances. It really is that simple.

There is nothing more liberating than embracing this extravagant truth. When we admit to the core of our being that our performance will never measure up to God's standard, then we can quit trying to make ourselves good enough and concentrate instead on having a *relationship* with him. Everything, absolutely everything — from my tendency to be selfish to why the snails won't leave my potted plants alone — is acceptable to talk to him about. And everything, absolutely everything, is reason to give him thanks and praise!

A relationship based on love for who I am and grace in spite of what I do causes me to melt in gratitude, humility, and tenderness. When I know that God looks beyond my performance to the woman he loves, I can't but sink into his embrace, recognizing yet again that it is this for which I thirst.

There is no one righteous, not even one.

ROMANS 3:10

❧

Lost and Found

THELMA WELLS

❧

*We have to realize that we cannot earn or win anything from God;
we must either receive it as a gift or do without it.*

OSWALD CHAMBERS

I've always been fascinated with one of the most colorful women in the Bible — Rahab, the heroine of
Jericho. Jericho was the key to the Israelites' conquest of
the Promised Land. If Joshua was going to defeat the
enemies of God's children in Canaan, he had to get Jericho first. The people of Jericho were keenly aware of this
and had fortified themselves with weapons and soldiers to
protect their city. Joshua had to send in spies to scope out
what the Israelite army would be up against if they tried
to take the city.

When Joshua sent two men from Acacia to spy on
Jericho, they went to Rahab's home. She was a woman of
ill repute, a prostitute. It was not unusual to see men
going in or out of her house. Little did anyone suspect that
Rahab the harlot had been tagged by God to play a special role in the unfolding of his plan.

Rahab welcomed the spies and hid them from the king
of Jericho and his men. When the soldiers came to

Rahab's house to ask about the men who had been there, Rahab said, "Yes, the men came to me, but I did not know where they had come from. At dusk, when it was time to close the city gate, the men left. I don't know which way they went. Go after them quickly. You may catch up with them" (Joshua 2:4–5).

Actually, the Jewish spies were hiding on the roof of Rahab's house at that very moment. But when Rahab sent the king's men in the wrong direction, they believed her story and hurriedly left to look for their enemies outside the city. In exchange for her courageous protection of them and her faith in their God, the spies struck a deal with Rahab, promising to spare her and her family when Joshua's army came back to destroy Jericho.

The thing that most fascinates me about this story is that God used this Canaanite woman, this black woman from the ancestry of Ham, this woman with a bad reputation and immoral profession, to prove that his grace is sufficient for anyone and everyone. His mercy is bestowed on all who repent. His salvation is freely given to all who confess him as Lord and receive him as Master of their lives. For her whole life, Rahab had been lost in the wilderness of sin. But now she was found by a loving heavenly Father who honored her heart and not only saved her life but named her proudly in the genealogy of Jesus Christ (Matthew 1:5; Hebrews 11:31).

You see, Sweetie, God makes no distinction on account of nationality, race, caste, or gender. He made us all and loves us equally. Christ came to remove every last wall of partition between us and his Father so that everybody who wants to can become part of his family. God's plan is for all of us to turn from our wicked ways and worship him like his daughter Rahab did. Even though we disobey his law, he has chosen to redeem us under the new covenant of Jesus Christ. As he rescued Rahab, not only from death but also from the clutches of her own sin, so he plans to rescue each one of us from our fate apart from him. "The Lord is not slow in keeping his promise, as some understand slowness. He is patient with you, not wanting anyone to perish, but everyone to come to repentance" (2 Peter 3:9).

Dear friend, if you are lost, you can be found. No one is destined for the "unclaimed" bin at life's Lost and Found. Simply acknowledge your need for the Savior and honor God as Rahab did. It doesn't matter who you are or where you've been. That's why grace is so amazing. It saves wretches like Rabab, like me, like you. Receive the gift, dear one. You are welcome in the family.

There is neither Jew nor Greek, slave nor free,
male nor female, for you are all one in
Christ Jesus.

GALATIANS 3:28

❧

Unwrapping
the Gift

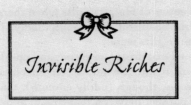

Invisible Riches

LUCI SWINDOLL

When we reach the end of our hoarded resources,
our Father's full giving has only begun.
ANNIE JOHNSON FLINT

Starting a day with laughter is my thing. So some years ago when I awakened from a dream, laughing, I was delighted.

I dreamed I was standing on a pile of fluffy clouds (in heaven, I guess), and somebody in a white robe presented me with a gift-wrapped box on a silver platter. The paper was bright with a huge bow on top. Colored confetti was scattered all around the gift. With great anticipation I opened it, but the only thing inside was a smaller box in the same kind of gift wrapping. So I opened it. Yet another box was there, smaller still. This went on box after box . . . until there were none. Each box had been beautifully wrapped, but was empty.

With ribbon and paper strewn at my feet, I turned to the white-robed figure and said, "There's nothing in the boxes."

He replied, "No . . . the gifts are there. Keep looking."

And then I woke up — laughing! I was mystified as to the dream's meaning. I'd been duped into believing I was receiving a series of fantastic gifts when there was nothing there but beautiful wrappings. Sadly, I will never know what the gifts were.

I've turned that dream inside out and upside down trying to figure it out. So far, I remain clueless. It has occurred to me, though (oddly enough), that there just might be a parallel between that dream and my life as a believer in Jesus Christ.

At the moment when we receive Christ as Savior, he presents us with his biggest gift of all: salvation by his grace. But inside that beautiful box are numerous other gifts from the Lord — all by-products of grace. With the human eye they can't be seen or touched, but they are real, nonetheless. And we spend our lifetime unwrapping them, one precious package at a time.

For example, there's the gift of forgiveness. We're exonerated from all our sins — past, present, and future — and we are given the strength and power to forgive others as we have been forgiven. We no longer have to carry around grudges that eat us alive.

There's the gift of imputed righteousness. This means that on the cross God poured our sins into Christ and Christ's goodness into us. Look at 2 Corinthians 5:21: "God made him who had no sin to be sin for us, so that in him we might become the righteousness of God." We are on all the right terms with God through his Son. When God looks at us, he sees his Child in us.

Then there's the gift of the indwelling Holy Spirit. This incredible gift is one of my favorites because I no longer have to work up the energy to do things that were God's to do in the first place. I don't have to always know the best course of action or figure out how I'm going to make ends meet. I have God's Spirit living in me and in my weakness, I can rely on his strength.

There's the gift of being my own priest. I don't go through another person to reach God's throne with my petitions. Rather, I have immediate access because I'm in Christ, who is seated at the right hand of God.

And there's the gift of eternal life. This isn't a concept, it's a person. "God has given us eternal life, and this life is in his Son. He who has the Son has life; he who does not have the Son of God does not have life" (1 John 5:11–12). These verses make it clear that Jesus himself is eternal life. This truth keeps me from getting bogged down with earthly circumstances and problems. The moment I place my trust in Christ, I am not given just a longer length of life but an entirely different quality of life. Forever.

Unlike my dream, the Christian life is not a stack of empty boxes. In Colossians 2:9–10, Paul writes, "For in Christ all the fullness of the Deity lives in bodily form, and you have been given fullness in Christ." Nothing empty about that! Because of grace incarnate, we have been given the limitless, ongoing, unmerited love of God. It takes us through life and into eternity.

Don't be duped into thinking that because you don't see it, grace isn't there. It is. Deity became humanity in order to bring it to us. It's new every day, just like packages waiting to be unwrapped on Christmas morning. Keep looking.

For you know the grace of our Lord Jesus Christ,
that though he was rich, yet for your sakes
he became poor, so that you through his
poverty might become rich.

2 CORINTHIANS 8:9

✌

Sloppy Living

MARILYN MEBERG

❦

In the cross there is safety.

THOMAS À KEMPIS

Many people tend to fear that if human behavior is not strictly monitored and restrained by the law, we will all simply run amok. Certainly we aren't to be trusted with the freedom and security grace offers to us; we're afraid that if we relax in that doctrine we will get in a mess.

I love the old German monk's contrasting statement to that fear: There is safety in the cross. The cross unwraps many promises and states of being for us. To list a few: it secures our salvation; it assures us of a place in heaven; it speaks of God's incomparable love for his children; and it releases us from the confines of the law and its impossible demands upon our behavior. And on top of all that, it keeps us safe from ourselves.

What do I mean by that? I'd like to suggest that safety comes from knowing a Father who not only loves and forgives by his inexhaustible grace but also instructs and disciplines when we get in a mess. First Peter 1 promises: "You call out to God for help and he helps — he's a good

Father that way. But don't forget, he's also a responsible Father, and won't let you get by with sloppy living" (THE MESSAGE).

Now if your humanity is anything like mine, you've probably tried your hand more than once at "sloppy living." But my safety, and yours, comes from knowing that God our Father keeps tabs on us and "won't let us get by" with living at a level below that to which he calls us. At some point, something or someone will come along as an instrument of God's love and discipline to lead us back to obedience. Never during that process is God's grace exhausted or his love extinguished. He simply manipulates our circumstances in such a way that our attention and direction are drawn back toward him. That knowledge of his steadfast commitment to keep us ultimately "on track" makes us feel secure . . . and keeps us safe.

A number of years ago when my first book, *Choosing the Amusing*, was released, I was invited to appear on the Jim Bakker television show to talk about the book. In an effort to acquaint myself more fully with that ministry, I began to watch the show. I found myself not quite trusting Bakker's television persona but at the same time touched by a subtle vulnerability that I sensed in him. A few weeks before I was due to fly to Charlotte for the program, Bakker's ministry collapsed under a barrage of moral and legal accusations that ultimately landed him in prison.

Bakker's experience has been an inspiring study to me in the steadying, disciplining hand of the Father as Jim's jail time led him from suicidal despair to repentance, victory, and, once again, ministry. Bakker maintains that the horror of his public humiliation, conviction, and incarceration was the best thing that ever happened to him. Through it all, Jim experienced the Father's refusal to let sloppy living take precedence over the call to obedience.

Jim learned the hard way, but in the learning he was held safely in the grip of his Father's sustaining grace.

John Piper, in his excellent book *Future Grace*, writes: "Sin is what you do when your heart is not satisfied with God. No one sins out of duty. We sin because it holds out some promise of happiness." When we swallow the lie that this life and its earthly experiences can provide greater enrichment and deeper happiness than following God, we're headed for sloppy living. We know better, but most of us don't live out of what we know; we live out of what we want. That sinful human characteristic makes God's extravagant grace even more astounding when we fully embrace it.

Grace frees us not only from the "never-being-good-enough" mindset but also from the fear that our sinful inclinations will ruin our life and sever our relationship with God. He has provided a place of safety for us . . . it's the Cross. That is where we go to confess our wrongdoing and to be reminded that our sin is not only forgiven but forgotten as well.

Friend, if you "know" in your head about the tenacious grace that keeps you safe but you need to *experience* it today in your life, dig a little deeper into the gift God has given you. Unwrap the treasure of the grace that will never let you go. A good Father never lets us get by with sloppy living. Experience that safety for yourself.

May the God of peace . . . equip you with all
you need for doing his will. May he . . . produce
in you . . . all that is pleasing to him.

HEBREWS 13:20–21 (TLB)

❧

4x4 . . . and I'm Not Talking My Hip Size

PATSY CLAIRMONT

❧

Amazing grace! How sweet the sound.

JOHN NEWTON

My spiffy new jalopy was parked in the driveway just waiting for me to unwrap it. It was the first new car I had picked out all by myself (like a big girl). A petite, sage-colored 4x4, the vehicle was equipped to take on the unsettled weather of Michigan and had just enough space in the back for my husband's electric cart that shuttled him effortlessly around malls and grocery stores. Les nicknamed his cart the Aarp Express, Aarpy, for short — referring to his card-carrying status as a member in the American Association of Retired Persons (AARP). I hadn't named my car yet.

When Les left on a week-long trip, my snappy wheels and I remained behind to get acquainted. I had only driven the vehicle a couple times. When Sunday morning rolled around, the day was frosty and flaky, and I headed out to drive my little darling to church. I started her up, and she purred like a kitten. What a sweet sound. After finally figuring out how to adjust my seat and strap on my seat belt, I tackled the defroster. This is when our relationship began to chill.

I couldn't find the right button. I did locate the sunroof button. About a quarter inch of fresh snow accumulated on my hairdo before I refound the sunroof button and shut the thing. But I couldn't find where the sick-o who designed the car had hidden my defroster button. Finally, using my fingernails, I scraped a four-by-six-inch opening on the windshield, turned on my wipers (which wouldn't stay on), and, grumbling, slid out of the driveway.

Within two blocks my four-by-six porthole had shrunk to a one-by-one peephole. I turned into a driveway to regroup (murmur, murmur). From the glove compartment I fished out the owner's manual. Printed across the book's cover in large letters was this message: "Read Manual Before Operating Vehicle." (Groan.)

That's the bottom line, folks: if we don't know how to unwrap and operate what we have, it will be of little value to us. We will be sidelined and left to fumble for the right buttons to push. I could tell from the outside that I had acquired a classy chassis, but I didn't understand the inside workings, which were vital to me if I was to benefit from all the vehicle had to offer.

The same is true of understanding God's workings. If we're not intimately familiar with his manual, what are the chances we'll understand his ways? Even reading the manual doesn't guarantee we'll comprehend the mystery of his plans, but at least we'll have a handle on which buttons to push in this life and which ones to avoid.

The Book will also help us to grasp grace as we study those who have gone before us. Living examples are some of the best learning aids. Take Abigail . . .

Old Testament Abby boarded her trusty, four-hoofed vehicle (her desert donkey) and headed out of her driveway. She wasn't on her way to church. Instead, she was bound for a colossal confrontation. Abigail was about to stand against 401 armed vigilantes who were on their way to her home to kill every man on the compound. This intelligent woman, who obviously had read the manual carefully, faced her enemies with courage and amazing grace — and turned them into friends. Abigail said all the right things. No grumbles, no groans, no murmurs. Imagine if she had pushed even one wrong button on those already outraged men. Why, Abby could have been their first casualty.

If you want an inside view of grace, if you want to see how to unwrap this astounding gift, take a closer look at Abigail, Hannah, Lydia, and Anna (whose very name means *grace*), and many of the other sisters who embraced grace long before we toddled onto the scene. Reading the manual makes sense. For who knows when loved ones may leave us, when winter may set in with a vengeance, or when enemies may pursue us, and we will need to know the sweet sounds of amazing grace.

Oh, by the way, I named my vehicle "Sassy."

The grace of the Lord Jesus be with you.

1 CORINTHIANS 16:23

❧

Been There, Done That

BARBARA JOHNSON

❧

Blessed are they who wallow in grace,
for they shall rise up in laughter.

*A*re you walking in the dark? Are the stars in your
universe covered by clouds? Is there no light at the
end of your tunnel — or do you see the headlight of an
oncoming train?

Be still. Get quiet. What's that you hear? In your darkest hours, listen to Jesus saying, "Been there. Done that!"

Jesus, by the grace of God, has tasted what you are
tasting, felt what you are feeling, looked into the black-
est pit and prayed, "My Father, if it is possible, may this
cup be taken from me" (Matthew 26:39). Jesus knows
the clutch of fear in the night, the pain of sharp rocks
under bare feet while dragging up a mountainside that
nobody walked before. He knows the sound of that whis-
tle from the oncoming train!

"Listen!" Jesus says. "Been there. Done that!"

Grace is God's gift in your darkness. Jesus is grace
personified. Are you going through a difficult struggle?
Sit down and hold God's gift of grace in your lap. Slowly
untie the ribbons. Now remove the lid on the box. Reach

beneath the tissue paper. It's party time! In the middle of your trial, God has prepared a celebration. Jesus triumphed over the worst, and now he will help you to do the same.

How will he do it? In a way you didn't expect. Jesus knows about everything you're going through, and he has made arrangements for you to look back on it — and laugh. He is going to bring laughter and liberty into your circumstances. Wherever Jesus is, there's a party going on. His grace is the yeast that makes hope and joy rise in your heart.

Do you wonder what makes me qualified to dispense this "theology of laughter"? The heat got turned up in my family over a nine-year period. I lost a son in Vietnam, and another to a drunk driver. My third son entered a life of homosexuality and was estranged from us for many years. It's been tough. Believe me, my struggles would make a perky geranium wilt. But you know what I learned? Grace is stronger than gravity! When you're falling down, down, down, it's not a question of how far you fall, but how high you bounce.

Developing my sense of humor and unwrapping grace daily helps me hang in there even when I don't get the answers I want. With Jesus beside me, I've learned to read the funnies of life and leave the rest of the newspaper lie. Now I blow the wrappers off straws, tie up little gifts to myself to unwrap on gloomy days, and dare to wear clothes that don't match. I've walked down the street dressed like an angel to deliver good news to someone. I've run through the sprinkler with clothes on. Sometimes I even eat dessert first because life is short ... but God's grace isn't.

Grace is all around you. No, life won't ever be perfect. Even in the land of milk and honey you can get kicked by a cow or stung by a bee. But when that happens, you can laugh with the Lord by your side and say with him, "Been there. Done that! I learned to embrace grace."

Thanks be to God for his indescribable gift!
2 CORINTHIANS 9:15

❧

Fresh Out of Grace?

BARBARA JOHNSON

Today is the tomorrow you worried about yesterday . . .
but not nearly enough.

*A*ll of us have times when we feel like running away from home. "Just the thought of *running* is enough to change my mind!" a friend told me. But there are better reasons for not running. Troubles are often the tools God uses to cultivate the fruit of his grace in our lives. Our challenge is to accept that grace, to obey, and to serve.

The widow at Zarephath accepted that challenge. In the account in 1 Kings 17, the prophet Elijah was hiding in a ravine when the brook dried up. The Lord said, "Go to Zarephath. . . . I have commanded a widow in that place to supply you with food" (verse 9). When Elijah got there, he found the widow and her son starving to death. She was preparing to make bread out of the last of their flour and oil that they might eat once more before dying.

Elijah asked the woman for a little water. He also asked for a little bread.

When she told him she had no bread, just a little oil and flour, he said, "Don't be afraid. Go home and do as you have said. . . . But first make a small cake of bread for me" (1 Kings 17:13).

Excuse me? I'm not sure I would have been gracious in those circumstances. But I guess the widow figured she had nothing to lose. Elijah promised her that if she followed his instructions, her jar of flour would not be used up and her jug of oil would not run dry.

So the widow did what Elijah asked her to do. And God graced her jug of oil and jar of flour. From then on, throughout the drought, there was sufficient food for Elijah, the widow, and her son.

Like the widow's oil, you can never use up grace. When you think you're fresh out of grace, God gives you more. When you use what you have, look at the jug — the more you use, the more you get!

After our son Larry disappeared into "the gay lifestyle," my mind was a blender full of emotions that whirled around and around. I loved Larry. I hated Larry. I wanted to kill him. I wanted to kill myself. I simply would not accept the idea that this thing had happened to our family.

Right around Mother's Day, mornings began looking extremely bad to me. I guess the thought of Mother's Day without Larry was more than I wanted to handle. After my doctor told me, "If he's been gone this long, it is very possible he will never come home again," I slipped into a zombie-like trance. Dr. Wells called my husband, Bill, and suggested having me put in a fine institution specializing in twenty-four-hour care for people who are suicidal. Bill told me he would make some calls to find out if his insurance would cover that.

I thought, *If Bill's insurance covers me, then I'm headed for Looney Tunes Haven. If it doesn't, then I'm supposed to stay home and count the roses on the wallpaper.*

Then the thought hit me: *Why toy with suicidal thoughts any longer? Why not go ahead and get it over with?* I got in my car, backed out of the driveway, and started down the street, not knowing where I was going. All I knew was that I couldn't go on like this.

As I headed up a viaduct, I intended to turn the wheel sharply to the right and plunge my car to the freeway below. *But what if that didn't finish the job?* I'd be crippled for life, making baskets — with lots of roses, of course. But I had to do *something*. I had given Larry to God many times, but I'd always taken him back. As I came over the top of the viaduct I thought, *Perhaps I could take a hammer out of my imagination and just nail Larry to the foot of the cross. That would do it! If I nailed my burden down, I couldn't pick it up again.*

I started down the other side of the viaduct, and that's exactly what I did. "Lord," I prayed, "I'm giving Larry to you once and for all. If he never comes home, it doesn't matter. If I never see him again, it doesn't matter. Whatever, Lord. I'm nailing that kid to the cross!"

The heavy, depressed feeling I had carried for so long evaporated. I sang all the way home.

I called Bill to explain my excitement. He was so surprised by the change in my voice, he told me not to call or talk to anybody until he got home. Eventually he understood and was relieved. He had learned that his insurance wouldn't have covered me anyway.

The next day, for the first time in over a year, I felt like cleaning house. I was vacuuming when the phone rang. It was Larry, wanting to know if he could come home to bring me a hamburger like he always used to do. Instead of saying, "You little creep, don't you know that they were ready to put me in the Home for the Bewildered?" I said, "Come on home, Honey." All I felt for my son was overwhelming love. I had finally embraced grace and learned what it means to let go in love.

What is it that *you* need today? Are you being tempted to despair? To throw in the towel? To lose hope? To roll over and die? God is watching in the wings. He says, "Bake a cake before you chuck it all." Face your fears. Unwrap the grace in this moment. Expect a miracle.

Friend, will you hoard the last drops of oil in your jug, or will you lavish them on others because you have nothing to lose? God has a plan. Be there when he stops by. Bake him a cake. He's got a miracle of grace in store, just for you.

> *Give, and it will be given to you. A good measure,*
> *pressed down, shaken together and running over,*
> *will be poured into your lap. For with the*
> *measure you use, it will be measured to you.*
>
> LUKE 6:38

❧

Stormy Weather

THELMA WELLS

❧

*Faith is a living, daring confidence in God's grace,
so sure and certain that a man would stake
his life on it a thousand times.*

MARTIN LUTHER

It was a beautiful, cloudless, calm afternoon on the beach at the Radisson Normandy Hotel in San Juan, Puerto Rico. It was the kind of day that makes you want to relax, read a good book, and soak in the sun. All conditions were right for a perfectly peaceful afternoon.

I settled into my beach chair with a good book, occasionally sipping tea through a red straw from a tall glass filled with ice chips, an orange wedge, a cherry, and a sprig of mint. Life was ever so sweet . . . for about an hour.

Suddenly the wind began to blow. The sky quickly changed from blue to gray to black. The storm was coming in so fast that I grabbed my book and my tea and hurried toward the verandah. I didn't make it. The rain started falling in sheets.

My greatest concern was my hair. See, I can't get my hair wet and shake it back to life like half the people in the world can. Black hair don't shake back, baby. You gotta go through a complex process to make it presentable.

Once I reached the verandah, I felt safer. I was a little disappointed, but I reasoned that I could still relax in a lawn chair on the verandah.

Just as I settled in and began reading, however, the wind changed direction. The rain started spraying in my face like water spewing out of a shower head.

Man! Dragging my drenched tail into my small, but elegant, hotel room, I flounced grumpily on the bed and demanded, "What's going on, Lord?" All I wanted was peace and quiet with birds chirping in the nearby trees and the sound of gentle waves rolling on the shore. Was that really too much to ask?

So now what should I do? I could go downstairs to the bar. But someone might think I was there to be picked up. I could go to the Plaza of the Americas and shop, but I had asked God to help get me out of credit card debt. Besides, I didn't really *need* anything. I could go to the restaurant again — the one I had just left. But they might think I had an eating (or drinking) disorder. Maybe I should just stay in my room and take a nap.

As I finished weighing my options, I looked out of the window and saw that as suddenly as the rains had come, the wind had ceased, the sun had returned, and all was calm again. And in the distant sky was a faint rainbow. Man!

That's the way it is with life. Things may be going well. You may be enjoying luxuries and success, prestige and power, good health and prosperity. Then storms roll in with sudden vengeance, and your ship begins to sink.

Jesus' disciples knew all about scary storms. One day Jesus and his friends set sail across the Sea of Galilee to relax. Suddenly, without warning, the winds changed and big waves began breaking over the boat, filling it with water. Frightened, the disciples went to Jesus, who was asleep in the back of the boat.

What! Asleep? They were indignant! Terrified! They woke him up and demanded to know, "Teacher, don't you care if we drown?"

Jesus was cool. He turned to the elements and said, "Quiet! Be still!"

Then he turned back to his disciples and asked two poignant questions: "Why are you so afraid?" And, "Do you still have no faith?" (Mark 4:37–40).

The disciples didn't get it. Even though they had been with Jesus when he had changed the water to wine, healed the sick, gave sight to the blind, and opened deaf ears, here they were allowing the wind and big waves to frighten them, even though the Savior was with them.

But don't be too hard on the disciples. Every day we are blessed with opportunities to unwrap God's grace in our scary moments. Every day we witness miracles that we know no human could perform — miracles like being able to breathe, walk, talk, move, see, think, taste, and touch. Evidence of God's presence and power is all around us in the universe — the sun, the stars, the birth of each new day. And yet, like Jesus' friends of old, we continue to search for peace outside of him, even when he is with us moment by moment on our journey. We sometimes ask the same question the disciples did: "Who is this?" (Mark 4:41).

Well, let's unwrap the gift he is to us.

> He's someone we can pray to.
> He knows what we need before we ask.
> He keeps his promises.
> He's our example.

He understands our tears.
He's always near.
He's our bridge over troubled waters.
He commands, "Quiet! Be still!"

When stormy weather rolls in around you, cry out to Jesus. No climactic change in your life is distressing or surprising to him. Listen to his still small voice as he whispers to you, "Why are you so afraid? Do you still have no faith?" When the gale is raging, you can be assured that he is standing by, speaking peace to your soul. Even the wind and the waves obey his will.

*Their ships are tossed to the heavens and sink
again to the depths; the sailors cringe in terror.
They reel and stagger like drunkards and
are at their wit's end. Then they cry to the Lord
and he saves them. He calms the storm and
stills the waves. What a blessing is that stillness
as he brings them safely into harbor.*

PSALM 107:26–30 (TLB)

❧

Box Seats Grace

MARILYN MEBERG

❧

A good sleep is grace and so are good dreams.
Most tears are grace.
The smell of rain is grace and somebody loving you is grace.

FREDERICK BUECHNER

In the California desert where I live, golf and tennis are big-time sports and attract top professionals from all over the world for competitive play. I was chomping at the bit to get seats for this year's Evert Cup, but the tennis event had been sold out for months. My dear friend and faith connoisseur extraordinaire, Ney Bailey, knew how much I wanted to go. On Tuesday evening she announced that she was going to get tickets for Wednesday.

I swallowed a derisive snort and tried tactfully to point out that the huge "sold out" sign at the tournament entrance had a pretty clear message. Without the slightest hint of spiritual superiority, Ney said, "I've been talking to God about this, Marilyn, so I'm going to the ticket window early in the morning to see what happens."

"See what happens?" I responded with more than a smidgen of skepticism. "Do you expect God to be there just waiting for a missionary type and her little-of-faith friend to show?" Ney smiled that serene smile of hers and told me to keep my phone line clear the next morning between 8 and 8:30.

The phone rang at 8:13 and a jubilant Ney announced that not only did she get seats, she got center court box seats. I let out a "Yahoo!" that I'm sure unsettled my neighbors. Within minutes I'd packed my hat, sunscreen, dark glasses, and water, and was out the door to meet my miracle-working friend.

As we waited for the first match of the day to begin, I asked Ney what God had looked like when he handed her the tickets. "Well, actually it was a woman in a green T-shirt who handed me the tickets," she said. We decided that image of God might not be well received in most Christian circles; perhaps it would be wise to keep this revelation to ourselves.

With great enthusiasm Ney then explained that some people had given up their box seats for that day with instructions for the folks at the ticket window to sell them. Because Ney was first in line, the seats were sold to her!

As the day progressed and we watched some of the finest tennis I'd seen in years, I kept saying to God, "Thank you, thank you, thank you! You know how I adore tennis . . . you know how I adore being outside in this gorgeous desert sunshine . . . you know I didn't want to be inside at my desk writing. I don't quite get it, but thank you, thank you, thank you!"

That evening as Ney and I were enjoying a late dinner, I once again shared with her what has been a spiritual conundrum to me most of my adult life: to what degree is God active in the minutia of daily living? I wobble back and forth on this issue. Of course I can and do talk to him about everything; that's part of maintaining my spiritual connection. And of course I know he loves me and cares about all facets of my experience. But tennis tickets ... do I really take *that* request to him? It almost seems like magical thinking to pray for tickets, and when we get them, assume God brought it about. It makes more sense to me that whoever owned those seats woke up with a debilitating sinus infection, thus freeing the seats for us.

As Ney and I tossed this subject around, she said something, as she has so many times in our twenty-two-year friendship, that made me suddenly very quiet at the center of my soul: "I learned years ago not to edit my prayers." She explained that her job is to "make her requests known," as a child would, and then, no matter the result, trust that God is praised and honored. "Like a father, it pleases him to give good gifts to his children," Ney said. "And Marilyn, God gifted both of us with a great day of tennis! Our job is simply to unwrap his gracious gift ... and enjoy!"

There was no way I could argue with that. But, you know, I can't help but feel bad for that person with the severe sinus infection.

And if you hardhearted, sinful men know how to give good gifts to your children, won't your Father in heaven even more certainly give good gifts to those who ask him for them?

MATTHEW 7:11 (TLB)

❧

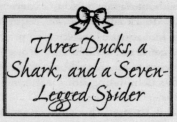

Three Ducks, a Shark, and a Seven-Legged Spider

SHEILA WALSH

∾

God gives the gifts where he finds the vessel
empty enough to receive them.

C. S. LEWIS

As I stood in my bathroom the other evening, I realized things had gotten seriously out of hand. It had started innocently enough. When my son, Christian, was born I purchased a set of three yellow ducks for his bath. It seemed like the thing to do. Small child = ducks in bath. But when his second birthday rolled around, he decided that he liked to take his baths in Mommy's and Daddy's bathtub — and of course the ducks came, too.

Then he added plastic versions of Barney, Baby Bop, and B.J., characters from one of his favorite television shows. Then came the seven-legged plastic spider he was given in the lobby of a hotel by the duty manager who was decorating for Halloween. I hoped Christian would lose it on the flight home, but old "Itsy Bitsy" appeared in our bath the next night. After our trip to Scotland to visit with Grandma Walsh we added Mommy Frog and Baby Frog from the aquarium gift shop just outside of Edinburgh.

Then "Papa" in Charleston took Christian to Chuckie Cheese, and a *big* shark and two small spiders were added to our dysfunctional aquatic family.

There was no end to the nightmare. Each evening as I would go to take my bath, I could see that the place was being gradually taken over. This one room in our house had once been a haven for me, but no more. Aromatherapy candles and soft music had been devoured by one lion, three frogs, three spiders, one panda bear, a hippo, a rhino, an elephant, three TV celebrities, a shark, a boat, four balls, a starfish, and a tiger. There was now officially no room for me.

One evening, just before bath time, Patsy called. We talked for a while, updating each other on the events of the week. Then I tried to describe to her the scene before me. "You should write about this!" she said. We chuckled, since we're always looking for fresh material for our books. But after we'd hung up, I thought about what she'd said and realized she was right. Here was a living parable of how my life so often becomes. *Cluttered.* I pick up "stuff" every day and carry it home with me, and soon there is no room left for the grace of God because my life is stuffed full. I want to live bathed in his grace, but I get so busy and so overwhelmed with "stuff" (inside and outside) that I miss the simple joy of resting in him, trusting him, enjoying his abundance. His gifts are all around me, but I don't unwrap them because I'm not aware of my need for what he offers.

Now don't get me wrong. I know God has given me much on this earth to enjoy — and I do! And I'm a big fan at heart of our waterlogged menagerie. I love the joy on Christian's face each evening as he gets ready for his bath. He knows that Mommy has already been in there and prepared the place. He looks at me and grins as he sees all his friends lined up along the side of the bath waiting for him in a long ... long ... long line. He picks up each one, says "hello," and throws it into the soapy deep. When he's finally fast asleep, I gather up all his stuff in his blue plastic boat and put it to one side, knowing his toys will reappear tomorrow ... but also knowing that for now they've served their purpose.

Perhaps there's a lesson for all of us there. The psalmist David writes that in the midst of the stress and confusion of everyday life, God has made known to him the path of life. He confidently asserts, "You will fill me with joy in your presence, with eternal pleasures at your right hand" (Psalm 16:11). But Lewis also reminds us that "God gives the gifts where he finds the vessel empty enough to receive them."

So each night now as I gather up my little lamb's bath mates and drop them into the boat, I also gather up the concerns and cares of the day that have filled my heart. Putting them to one side, I make room for Christ, the incarnation of grace. I stop to take notice of the gift of his presence. And he fills me with joy as I unwrap the treasure.

You have made known to me the path of life; you will fill me with joy in your presence, with eternal pleasures at your right hand.

PSALM 16:11

❧

Granny's Grace

Thelma Wells

❧

We are raised high in God's sight through his grace. . . .
For our courteous Lord does not wish his creatures to lose hope
even if they fall frequently and grievously; for our failure
does not prevent him from loving us.

Julian of Norwich

When I was a little girl, I lived in an apartment with my great-great-grandmother, Grandma Mollie; Granny, my great-grandmother who raised me; and my great-grandfather, Daddy Harrell. Across the front of the entire apartment building was a screened-in front porch, and a long flight of stairs extended from our apartment to the yard below.

One sunny, hot day, I was sitting on the porch talking to Daddy Harrell. Granny was working in her flower garden downstairs, and Grandma Mollie was enjoying her afternoon tobacco. When Grandma Mollie decided it was time to spit, she strolled to the top of the stairs, leaned over the wooden banister, and spewed a big wad of snuff.

It landed smack dab on top of my kneeling granny's head.

Granny screeched so loud, I bet everyone in the next county heard her. "Mama!" she hollered. "Can't you see I'm down here? You spit that stuff in my hair! What'cha doing spitting off the banister anyway? You got a spit can! I just washed my hair and now I've got to wash it again. I'm so mad at you I don't know what to do. Get back in the house. I don't even want to look at you right now!"

Grandma Mollie was soooo embarrassed. She hadn't even looked down when she stepped up to the banister. All she'd been thinking about was emptying her mouth of that accumulation of snuff. Stunned and hurt by her daughter's harsh words, Grandma Mollie slowly walked back into the house with tears beginning to trickle down her beautiful, high cheekbones.

"I didn't see her," she lamented. "I never would've done that if I'd seen her. I love her! I just didn't see her."

Mad Granny swept swiftly up the stairs with garden dirt on her hands and snuff spit on her head. By the time Granny reached the front door of the apartment, Grandma Mollie was crying openly, I was crying, and Daddy Harrell was pleading.

"Sweetie," he said, "don't be mad at Mollie. Don't be hard on her. She didn't see you. She didn't mean it. Can't you see she's as hurt as you are? Come on now, wash your hair and get over it. Sweetie, look at your mama. She's hurting because of this."

Granny looked at her mother's hurt, distraught, apologetic face, and tears of compassion began to flow down her brown, round cheeks, lapping under her double chin. In that moment I saw in my Granny's eyes a love for her mother that words cannot express.

With the snuff still in her hair and dirt underneath her fingernails, Granny knelt at her mother's feet as Grandma

Mollie sat in the old dark brown velveteen rocker. Granny laid her head in Grandma's lap and said, "Mama, I know you didn't mean it. I forgive you!"

What a gift! Pardon and reconciliation. Grandma Mollie unwrapped it with relief and joy.

I learned something that day about the way our Father God deals with us. Daddy Harrell showed me how Jesus, who is sitting at the right hand of his Father making intercession for us, pleads for sinners: "They're sorry, Father. Have mercy on them." My granny, willing to hear the plea of "guilty" and respond with such tenderness and pardon, was a picture of what a gracious God offers us all. We step to the banister of our lives, fail to consider the consequences of what we're about to do, and spit our selfish desires in the face of Jesus. Once we realize what we've done, we begin to plead for mercy and forgiveness. Even though he's hurt and grieved about what we've done, he listens to our plea, wraps us in his loving embrace, and grants us unmerited favor — grace that is greater than all our sin. That day on the porch I saw myself in Grandma Mollie — a recipient of the gift of grace.

Do you need grace today, my friend? Pardon and reconciliation? Amazing grace is the kind of grace we sing about. It is yours for the unwrapping. Accept the gift. Open it with joy!

*Yet he, being compassionate, forgave their
iniquity, and did not destroy them; he restrained
his anger often, and did not stir up all his wrath.*

PSALM 78:38 (RSV)

❧

Eyes to See

SHEILA WALSH

&

Let never day or night unhallowed pass,
but still remember what the Lord has done.

WILLIAM SHAKESPEARE

Sometimes we are gifted with moments of grace that take us by surprise. I had such a moment at Christmastime 1998. Barry, Christian, and I flew home to Scotland to celebrate our lamb's second birthday with his Scottish grandma. It was Christian's first overseas flight, nine hours during the night. In an attempt to make the trip less stressful for Christian (and for us) we decided to use our upgrades and get free first-class tickets.

We felt like the cat's pajamas as we sailed on board! Christian floated into first class like he had been born to it. He had his own seat. He had his own video player with cartoons and *Annabelle's Wish* ... the movie! He had his own cool little toilet bag. We got him into his pj's, said our prayers, kissed him good-night, and settled back for our fifteen-course gourmet meal.

"This is really going to work," I said to Barry. "This is great. He'll sleep. We'll sleep. We'll arrive in London refreshed and ready to go."

Ha! Ha! Ha! He slept for twenty minutes. All I got of the fifteen-course meal was the nuts!

I tried to work out why Christian couldn't sleep. "Are your ears sore?" I asked.

"No."

"Is your mouth sore?"

"No."

"Do you want to go back to sleep?"

"No!"

We spent the next eight hours and forty minutes walking him up and down — in coach.

We were due to land at London's Gatwick Airport at 7 A.M. Thirty minutes before touchdown, Christian finally decided to rest quietly on my lap. We took our seats in first class again and looked out the window as the sun began to rise over the lovely green fields of England. It was one of those glorious winter mornings when the frost sparkles on the grass like Christmas lights. I could see herds of cows congregated around old trees as if they were discussing their holiday plans. Scattered over the rolling hills were flocks of sheep, just as on that first Christmas morning. The scene was like a quaint Victorian Christmas card.

I smiled, remembering so many mornings like this when I was a student at London Bible College. I would get up early, pull on a heavy coat and boots, and head out into the crisp air. I loved it when my footprints were the first to touch the freshly frosted sidewalks. Some of my most intimate times with God as a student were spent on those cold winter mornings before the rest of London (certainly any London student) was awake.

I looked down now at the little monkey on my lap. He had his head on my shoulder, thumb in his mouth. The morning sun picked out the gold highlights in his hair. He looked almost angelic! I drank in that moment of grace, decorated with memories of gracious moments from the past.

The flight had not been what I had hoped for. My expectations sat at my feet like discarded, disappointing gifts. But there was a different treasure here. Instead of being fast asleep as we were deposited gently on British soil, I enjoyed the gift of that winter wonderland morning as I sat beside my loving husband and delightful little rascal of a son, reflecting with gratitude on the daily walks I'd had with Christ as a young woman, when I was nineteen.

I can so easily dismiss moments like these because they are not on my list. They aren't the gifts I asked God for. But grace is a surprise package. If I'm not open, I miss it altogether.

Grace is with us every day, whether in the carpool with four noisy six-year-olds or on a flight with one cranky two-year-old. Grace is always available for the unwrapping. I am praying for new eyes for next Christmas — eyes to see and enjoy unexpected moments of grace in everyday life.

Every day I will praise you and extol your name
for ever and ever. Great is the LORD and most
worthy of praise; his greatness no one can fathom.

PSALM 145:2–3

Present-Moment Grace

BARBARA JOHNSON

❧

*Yesterday is a canceled check. Tomorrow is a
promissory note. Today is cash. Spend it wisely.*

At our local post office there is a huge clock that
shows the days, hours, minutes, and seconds until
the millennium. The first time I waited in line and
watched those seconds tick by, I became more conscious
than ever of how brief life is. Psalm 90:10 reminds us,

"The length of our days is seventy years — or eighty, if
we have the strength; yet their span is but trouble and sorrow, for they quickly pass, and we fly away."

How briskly the hours and days speed by! What a
tragedy that most of us spend fifty-nine minutes of
every hour living in the past. At the beauty shop this
week the receptionist greeted me with a sad face. She
said, "My sister died forty-one years ago today, and I
remember her death whenever the date comes around."
I thought, *How much healthier to rejoice in her life and the
years you shared with her than to mourn all over again, year
after year!*

We waste so much time nursing regrets over lost jobs
or soured relationships; we harbor shame for things

poorly done. But dwelling on what cannot be changed will only steal our precious joy today.

Renee Katz was a young musician who played flute and piano until she was pushed from a New York City subway platform. Her right hand was severed by an oncoming train. No longer able to play a musical instrument, she has become an occupational therapist and a singer. "I've learned to use the insights I gained," she says, "and not just feel that life cheated me."

That is grace!

To face a titanic hour with cool calm is grace. To speak words of wisdom when the boat is sinking is grace. And to swim in deep waters of adversity rather than drown in despair is grace. When things go slow, go bad, go sour, or go away, it's time to unwrap the life preserver of God's love and stay afloat on the boundless ocean of his grace.

But don't wait for catastrophe before you unwrap grace. Embrace it *today*. Remember, friend, the past is gone. The future is unknown. There is only one minute in which you are alive. This minute! Right here, right now.

Here are some grace-filled things you could do today to make the world sing a sweeter song:

- Take a friend to lunch, and laugh.
- Record five things for which you are grateful.
- Call your mother and give her some good news.
- Pick a bouquet of dandelions, daisies, or delphiniums — even if you have to get them from a florist.
- Share a funny joke with your neighbor.
- Play your favorite music before you go to sleep.
- Pay attention to detail.
- Prepare for adventure.

Open your heart and your present moments to God's extravagant grace. Unwrap it in troubled times. Appreciate it *now*.

And my God will meet all your needs according to his glorious riches in Christ Jesus.

PHILIPPIANS 4:19

❧

Appreciating
the Gift

Anyone Seen Betty?

MARILYN MEBERG

~

*Atonement: it means exactly what it says: at-one-ment.
There is nothing about crime and punishment in the make-up
of that word. It simply means to be at one with God.*

MADELEINE L'ENGLE

Not long ago a woman named Betty corralled me after a conference and confided: "You know what I just love about the God in the New Testament? He's just so much more pleasant than that one in the Old Testament. What I mean is, the modern God is so much more liberal . . . I mean liberal about the sin stuff and everything. You know that woman at the well that Jesus was chatting with . . . you know, the one who moved through husbands like I do cheesecake? Well, Jesus was so nice about all that. And then of course there's that woman doing you know what *right in the middle of the day*. And Jesus didn't even have a fit about it! I love that about him."

I wonder if Betty's sentiments are more common than we might think. Quite frankly, I understand right where she's coming from. Sunday school, church, and vacation

Bible school were all a part of my life as I grew up, and I can vividly remember thinking that the stories I heard about how God wiped out whole cities including women and children was scary. I was convinced he was powerful, but never in a million years would I believe he was pleasant.

As I grew older I decided not to read the Old Testament at all. If I were to be perfectly honest then, I thought God was arrogant, narrow-minded, and barbaric. Of course I never admitted that to a living soul, and I certainly didn't tell God! I didn't want to risk being struck by a plague!

During my junior year at Seattle Pacific University I had one of those "aha" moments in the middle of Dr. Demaray's class on evangelism. He pointed out that in the Old Testament, God was graphically illustrating his utter intolerance of sin. That's why those people who lived in total disobedience were wiped out. The law was: you sin, you're warned, you don't heed the warning, you die!

Dr. Demaray went on to explain that when Jesus became the embodiment of the world's sin, God, who cannot tolerate sin, turned momentarily away, thus provoking the anguished cry, "My God, my God, why have you forsaken me?" It wasn't that God's heart was indifferent to the death of his son; he simply cannot compromise his holiness by even looking on sin.

It began to make more sense to me why God seemed so inflexible about sinful people, but it still made him a bit scary. It took a few more years for me to finally fit the Old Testament God and the New Testament God into one integrated, harmonious whole.

That all happened when I joined a Bible study on the book of Romans and finally learned the meaning of justification. This is the truth that can free you from those crabby inner voices that tell you you're still a sinner in spite of having received Jesus as Savior, and God might zap you anyway simply because he's ticked off at you. It will also give you the whole picture of God: not only is he powerful, he is indeed pleasant!

Romans 5:1 states, "Therefore, since we have been justified by faith, we have peace with God through our Lord Jesus Christ." Chuck Swindoll clearly defines this extravagant gift of justification through God's grace.

> It is the sovereign act of God whereby He declares righteous the believing sinner while still in his sinning state. It doesn't mean that the believing sinner stops sinning. It doesn't even mean that the believing sinner is made righteous in the sense of suddenly becoming perpetually perfect. The sinner is declared righteous. God sovereignly bestows the gift of eternal life on the sinner at the moment he believes and thereby declares him righteous while the sinner still lives a life marked by periodic sinfulness. God takes the guilty, believing sinner who says "I am lost, unworthy, guilty as charged, and undeserving of forgiveness" and extends the gift of eternal life because Christ's death on the cross satisfied His demands against sin, namely death. And God sees the guilty sinner (who comes by faith alone) as righteous as His own Son.

Do you realize what this means? Even though we still sin and often can't seem to stop, God declared us righteous when we believed and received Jesus. And because the sin thing stays with us like onions after lunch, we desperately need God's grace. We deserve to be overtaken by locusts, but instead we're embraced by forgiveness and

miraculously accepted as righteous by the very God who
will not tolerate wrongdoing of any kind!

I realize now that without knowing God's utter intolerance of sin, I could never begin to appreciate how incredible
is the grace with which he embraces me. The God of the Old
Testament is the *same* God who ordained the Cross of forgiveness and grace.

Someone needs to explain all that to Betty.

> *Through [Christ] we have gained access by faith*
> *into this grace in which we now stand. And we*
> *rejoice in the hope of the glory of God.*
>
> ROMANS 5:2

ᴇᴅ

Tongue-Tied

LUCI SWINDOLL

❧

God loves old ordinary me, even or especially
at my most scared and petty and mean and
obsessive. Loves me; chooses me.

ANNE LAMOTT

When I moved to California twenty-five years ago, I often went with Marilyn to hear her speak. One fall day we were heading home when we both spotted a sign: "Fresh Apple Pie. Turn here." We did.

There was quite a crowd gathered in line for pie. Among those waiting was a large, tough-looking, loud-mouthed woman wearing a uniform. She ordered several pieces of pie. I assumed she was going into the bush to chow down with the militia. We both commented on how loud and rude she was, yelling at several little Boy Scouts who were enjoying themselves too much on her shift.

After getting our pie, we joined about thirty people, all strangers, and enjoyed chatting, eating, and drinking coffee. Suddenly, Loud Mouth came into the center of the circle, holding a piece of pie and yelling, "DAVIIIIIIID! DAVID! Get over here right now!" All eyes turned as David, about seven, hurried up to her with his arms out to take the pie.

"When I call you, you answer me. DO YOU HEAR ME?" She proceeded to hit David in the head, knocking his cap off and his pie into the dirt.

I was stunned. Horrified. Speechless.

We all stopped eating, talking . . . breathing. Momentarily, out of the silence, we heard a lone, stern voice say, "You hit that child one more time, and you'll have to deal with me."

I was dumbfounded. It was Marilyn; tender, gracious, unarmed Marilyn. *Are you crazy?* I thought. *Loud Mouth is going to make mincemeat out of you.*

Let me remind you, this was twenty-five years ago. Child abuse was not the issue it is today. I had never seen a child abused in a public place, and I'd certainly never seen anyone defend or protect a stranger's child. I was sure Marilyn was going to be decked, if not destroyed.

But nothing happened. Marilyn's gaze was fixed on the woman, the woman stared back, everyone in the crowd looked at each other, and I crawled under a rock, mortified. You see, I believe in minding my own business. And that's my preference for everyone. I was concerned about the child, but I was more concerned about seeing my dear friend clobbered in broad daylight.

No further words were exchanged, but a heavy pall hung over the place. As we began to disperse, various people came up to Marilyn to say, "I admire you for doing that." Or, "I never could have stood up to that woman, but it was great that you did." Some folks simply said, "Thank you."

The more I listened to these comments, the more conflicted I felt inside. I'd chosen to do what comes naturally to me. I'd decided to say nothing. I'd even wanted Marilyn to stay silent. But I was wrong. Dead wrong. I didn't have the courage to openly defend that little boy even though I knew his scout leader was brutally off base. I was afraid of what might happen if I spoke up . . . if anybody spoke up. I was afraid of what would happen to me. My apprehension struck me mute.

There resides in the heart of every believer little pockets of fear. For some of us it's cowardice. For others, it's timidity. Although we know the Savior gives courage and power, sometimes we feel safer in our little pocket than in his big provision. So we cower inside, afraid to be bold. We permit our human frailty to stand in the way of his strength.

Amazingly though, God has grace for this kind of behavior. He understands our weaknesses. Just because Marilyn spoke up and I didn't, that doesn't mean he likes her better than he does me. I take such comfort in that because even in my most unbecoming, inept, self-loathing moments, God still loves me with all his heart. When my weakness prevails rather than his strength, he doesn't condemn me. He doesn't compare me to Marilyn. Now when I come face-to-face with my less-than-perfect behavior, instead of condemning or comparing, I'm learning to lean on him and pray, "Lord, make me more like you. When I want to retreat, give me your courage." He longs to, and he does.

To me this fact is one of the most remarkable aspects of God's character. He chooses me because he *wants* to. And he changes me. Makes me more like I wish I were. More like him.

But you, O Lord, are a compassionate and
gracious God, slow to anger, abounding in love
and faithfulness. Turn to me and have mercy on
me; grant your strength to your servant.

PSALM 86:15–16

𝒶

I Blew It

THELMA WELLS

❧

He will continually follow you with his favours,
and not let slip any opportunity to be gracious to you.

MATTHEW HENRY

My friend in Arizona sent me an "IMPORTANT" e-mail that needed immediate action. The message said that Christians had allowed the famous atheist Madalyn Murray O'Hare to remove prayer from school and that now she was working to get Christian radio and television off the airwaves. The Federal Communications Commission had scheduled a hearing in Washington, and more than 287,000 names had already been registered approving the elimination of Christian programming. One million signatures were needed to stop this proceeding! A form letter was attached to the e-mail asking that every adult in the family sign the letter individually and that we also get our churches, neighbors, and friends to sign and send copies of the letter in protest.

Being the advocate for Christian programming on radio and television that I am, I was not about to stand back and watch this kind of thing happen again! I organized my staff to prepare 2,000 of these letters and get them in the mail that very day.

Late Friday evening, after the big push to get this information into the hands of thousands before Sunday morning so they could present this information to their churches, I received a phone call from a friend asking three simple questions:

1. Has Madalyn Murray O'Hare been found? (She had been missing for more than three years.)
2. When is the hearing scheduled?
3. Is there a specific person to send the letter to?

I promptly got back on e-mail and queried my friend in Arizona. This was her reply:

Dear Thelma,

I am soooo sorry! I recently found out the Madalyn Murray O'Hare information is a hoax! I received the e-mail from a credible source and just assumed they had checked into it. I tried to remember who all I had forwarded that e-mail to so I could let everyone know that this information is not true, but obviously I forgot that I'd sent it to you. I've learned my lesson, and am going to research more thoroughly before forwarding any more e-mails similar to this!

My stomach dropped to my feet. My head starting pounding. No! No! How could I have been so gullible? Why didn't I check out the story for myself? What have I done? What will people think when they discover I sent them down the wrong path?

I prayed, "Lord, show me how to handle this because you know the damage I've done. At least 2,000 people have been sent erroneous information. Just think how far it can spread!"

Karole, my administrative assistant, had worked like mad to get the letters out. I just knew she was going to be upset because I had taken her off another important project to complete this one. But when I broke the news to her, she just said, "Oh, that's all right. I only got 600 letters sent out on Friday. The other 1,400 letters are still in my office. I know who the 600 are . . . all I have to do is send them an apology."

Whew! God, in his infinite wisdom and mercy, saved us from the overwhelming embarrassment and expense of my misguided zealousness.

As Christians, we have responsibility to seek out the truth and know it for ourselves. How often do we misinterpret and misquote Scripture because we fail to go to the Bible and understand its message? How often have we led people down the wrong path because of our actions and words? It is by the grace of God that we are able to work through these situations without doing irreparable damage.

God knew the potential results of my actions before I did and graciously conceived a time delay in disseminating my "urgent" message. That's grace! My goal was to STOP THIS RIGHT NOW — by my own efforts. But who am I, without God's clear direction, to try to stop anything? I blew it. God hindered it. Grace covered it. What a gift!

When we open our eyes to the gift of grace each day, we discover that God is always working behind the scenes of our lives, covering our tracks when we hook up the cart before the horse . . . when we are so determined to do right that we fail to be reasonable.

*Great are the works of the LORD; they are pondered
by all who delight in them. Glorious and majestic are
his deeds, and his righteousness endures forever.
He has caused his wonders to be remembered; the
LORD is gracious and compassionate.*

PSALM 111:2–4

❧

Momo's Magic

LUCI SWINDOLL

❧

Man is born broken. He lives by mending.
The grace of God is glue.
EUGENE O'NEILL

My maternal grandmother was wonderful. Sometimes I wish she were around today because she'd
be up for anything fun or enterprising or adventuresome.
We called her "Momo," and she loved the nickname.

Extremely musical (having taught piano for more than
thirty years), Momo sang in the church choir, was a big-
time party-giver, and an inveterate storyteller. She never
missed anybody's birthday, kept journals and scrapbooks
all her long life, and insisted on bringing a huge bunch of
folk home for a big dinner after church almost every Sunday. "What's one more mouth to feed?" she'd say. "We'll
just add another bean to the pot."

Momo's indomitable sense of humor saw her through
life's tough situations and brought joy to her four children
and many grandchildren. I still miss her even though she's
been with the Lord forty-six years.

On my tenth birthday, Momo gave me a new shiny
blue bicycle — my first. I was ecstatic. My brothers each

had one, so naturally I wanted one, too. Envisioning myself with an inherent riding ability, I was outside at dawn's early light to engage in what was going to become "my sport." I lifted my leg to get on my new steed. Just then the wheels moved forward, and I fell. Clearly, this bike-riding business looked a lot easier than it was.

I tried again. And again. There was something about moving forward while staying seated that seemed like patting your head and rubbing your stomach at the same time. I couldn't get the hang of it. After an hour of failure to even get on the seat, I threw the bike against the big oak tree and stormed inside.

Later I tried again and the results were much the same. The bike simply didn't want to be ridden. After several more attempts I finally mounted it, wobbled about two feet, only to have my pants leg catch in the drive chain. Falling off once again, I furiously tugged at the cloth and the chain, getting oil on my hands and a rip in my pants. Huffing and puffing, I threw the bike against the tree. Again.

After several days, the bike and tree were quite bonded, and I was a living hornet's nest. That bicycle hated me . . . and the feeling was mutual. A week into this standoff, Momo asked how I was progressing and said she'd like to watch me ride. Little did she know her gift was now a crooked heap of metal, with wheels out of alignment, bent frame, scuffed handlebars, and dirty seat that was almost twisted off. Uh-oh.

Defeated, I pushed the bike over to Momo's house and told her how bad I felt because I couldn't ride . . . that I was a failure, and was sorry for the mess I'd made. I cried and asked her to forgive me. She looked at the bike (if I remember correctly, her eyes did sort of roll), then at me, and said, "Honey, anything's hard when you first start out, but be patient. You'll get the hang of it before long; then it'll be fun. Don't give up."

That encouragement from my grandmother was just the inspiration I needed to press on. The next day I actually rode about five minutes without falling. The bike and I were both wobbling along, but I hung in there. There was something about Momo believing in me that held me on that wobbly seat and propelled me forward. I've been an avid bike rider ever since.

Sometimes God gives us gifts that are hard for us to enjoy or appreciate so we misuse them. He graces us with a day of rest apart from the turmoil, but instead of enjoying his soothing presence we fill the quiet with television or mindless activity. He sends a friend to support us when we're blue, but because it isn't exactly who we want to be with we brush her off and miss the gift. He gives us an opportunity to forgive, but we cling to our bitterness and hold on to the grudge. He offers us a chance to be taught something new, but we're too proud to learn. The list goes on.

We need to recognize how often we mistrust the Lord and reject his gracious gifts because they're not on our terms. Then we can tell him how disappointed we are. He meets us in our honesty, mends us with his grace, and pours the oil of his love all over us. Even if things are still not in perfect alignment, we're able to move forward.

This is what the LORD says, he who made the earth, the LORD who formed it and established it—the LORD is his name: "Call to me and I will answer you and tell you great and unsearchable things you do not know."

JEREMIAH 33:2–3

On the Road Again

SHEILA WALSH

❧

If and when a horror turns up you will then be given
Grace to help you.
I don't think one is usually given it in advance.

C. S. LEWIS

When my son Christian was born, Barry's parents, Eleanor and William Pfaehler, were so far over the moon you could only see them on a very clear night. My husband is their only child. For twelve years they had prayed and waited for a baby. When Barry finally arrived, he was welcomed like rain on a parched desert. So when Eleanor's "baby" had a baby, the joy was almost more than she could contain.

Eleanor never imagined that she would live to see that day. Before Barry and I were married she had three heart attacks and was not expected to survive. But she did. "How I prayed that God would spare me to see my only child married and happy," she would often tell me when they came to visit us in our first home. Then at forty I became pregnant! I think she upped her tithe to fifty percent! What a joy it was to place that darling little boy, her only grandbaby, into her arms and see the look of wonder and fulfillment on her face.

I began traveling with Women of Faith when Christian was six weeks old. Before my first trip Eleanor asked, "What are you going to do with the baby when you're on stage?"

"One of the local churches is providing a baby-sitter," I explained. Eleanor didn't sound too thrilled, but Christian and I set off anyway.

When the pastor's wife ushered a young girl into my dressing room and introduced her as the baby-sitter, I was stunned. Rooted to the spot. The girl looked to be about five years old, with purple fingernails the length of California. She was chewing enough gum to pull out every tooth in my head. I paid her and sent her home.

"This is not going to work," I said to Barry on the phone, tears streaming down my face. "I can't leave him with a total stranger who looks like she's been out of diapers for four weeks."

That's when Eleanor stepped in. "We'll come," she said.

"To every conference?" I asked.

"Yes, to every one."

Now, I have been an international traveler for years. It's amusing to my family in Scotland that the ten-year-old girl who couldn't ride for more than two miles in a car without throwing up grew into someone who now has more frequent-flyer miles than the Archangel Gabriel!

For three years I traveled across Europe with Youth for Christ. I have flown to Hong Kong, Indonesia, Singapore, and Malaysia with Youth With A Mission. At one point I had more than half a million frequent-flyer miles on United Airlines. I'm sure I was in line for a free jumbo jet. I've taken bands on the road, new books or CDs on the road, purchased new outfits for the road. But it's quite another thing to take cancer on the road. That's what my mother-in-law did during the last two years of her life. Anytime Christian wasn't with me or Barry, he was with his nana and papa.

Perhaps you're thinking that every grandmother would love to see that much of her grandchildren. I'm sure that's true, but not every nana has liver cancer. I know that there were many weekends when Eleanor did not feel like getting on a plane and heading hundreds of miles away from home, but I watched as she refused to stay in bed and embraced grace for every difficult step. She could have sat at home in greater comfort, close to her own doctors if she needed them, but she chose instead to step out in faith. She gave sacrificially to all of us, and in doing so, she told me, experienced more of the grace and provision of God than she had known in her life before.

That's the mystery of the gift of grace. It shows up just when you need it. Not a moment too soon, but not a moment too late. We can live our lives nailed to a spot by fear, or we can reach out beyond ourselves and find a well of grace springing up just where we need it most.

I'm sure Eleanor had read the psalmist's words many times before, but when she took cancer on the road she *knew*: "The salvation of the righteous comes from the LORD; he is their stronghold in time of trouble" (Psalm 37:39).

> *God is our refuge and strength, an ever-present help in trouble. Therefore we will not fear, though the earth give way and the mountains fall into the heart of the sea, though its waters roar and foam and the mountains quake with their surging.*
>
> PSALM 46:1–3

❧

No Guts, No Glory

PATSY CLAIRMONT

❧

Grace under pressure.
ERNEST HEMINGWAY

Grace under pressure" was Hemingway's response when someone asked him what he meant by the word *guts*.

What an elegant definition for such a sweaty, life-wrenching word. I tend to think of a word like *grace* as a woman's word, and a word like *guts* as a guy's word. But the truth is, Mike Utley was a picture of grace when he faced the toughest tackle life could challenge him with, and he stood to take another step.

Les and I sat with our eyes glued to the television as the big, strapping ex-football player took hold of the forearms of two of his teammates, using them as balance bars. With their help and his determination, he stood to his feet and prepared to take his first step in seven years. The man, Mike Utley, had been injured in a football game. Since severely damaging, but not severing, his spinal cord, he fought his way back to health. Seven years of grueling physical therapy. Seven years of maintaining an "I can do it" attitude.

I remember when Mike was carried out on a stretcher, and I remember breathing a prayer on his behalf. Les and I followed up on news reports about Mike's injury until, after a time, more current events filled the airways. Then our own challenges filled our minds and, quite honestly, we hadn't thought about Mike for a long time. But when the newscast showed him taking his first step, we watched in admiration as Mike dedicated himself to the task before him. Jaw set, eyes focused on his goal, with support people in place around him, the giant clutched his friends, and with tremendous courage and all the guts he could muster, he took his step. Exhausted from the effort, he was lowered back into a wheelchair. What a gutsy man!

Our willingness to embrace grace is more difficult when it's depicted in such a costly manner. But grace wasn't the injury Mike sustained; the injury was simply life's parcel. Grace was Mike's ability to accept wherever life took him and to continue to move forward.

This grace was evident in Joseph's life as well. Joseph was rejected and abandoned by his brothers, then falsely accused and imprisoned by his employer. He sat forgotten in jail for years. What a potential breeding ground for hostility, resentment, and anger! But instead of steeping in self-pity or seething in indignation, Joseph became an exemplary prisoner and a trusted leader in the jail. Forgotten by others, but not by God, Joseph was granted unmerited favor in his captors' eyes. Eventually, Joseph was released and elevated to the second highest in command over Egypt.

I believe God's fortitude and grace sustain the Josephs and the Mikes, the Josephines and the Michelles of this world. Even the Patsys.

For I, too, was a prisoner, an emotional prisoner. For several years I was held hostage in my home by fear and anger. Not knowing how to deal with the inequities of life, I stuffed my splintered emotions. Unlike Mike or Joseph, I wasn't courageous, nor did I know how to handle life's pressures. Still, in my extreme weakness, God extended his grace to me. I embraced grace like a balance bar and gradually got back on my feet. Then with my jaw set and my eyes focused, I took the first gutsy steps out of my home.

God wants you to experience his grace whether you have faced your life with courage or with cowardice. Grace is not about us; it is about God. He will meet you wherever you are to help you take the next gutsy step. Understanding God's grace and appreciating it will change your approach to life's pressures. You will begin to see the injustices as opportunities for you to watch God at work.

By the way, God is not often in a hurry to move us on before we benefit deeply from our experiences. So don't be disheartened when others forget your long, hard struggles. He will never forget . . . and his grace will exalt you in due time.

*You then . . . be strong in the grace that is
in Christ Jesus. . . . Endure hardship with us
like a good soldier of Christ Jesus.*

2 TIMOTHY 2:1, 3

❧

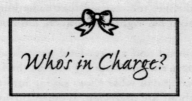

Who's in Charge?

THELMA WELLS

God is gracious to whom he will be gracious.
He is not limited by anyone's wickedness. He is never
trapped by his own wrath. His grace may
break out anywhere he pleases.

JOHN PIPER

*W*hat an honor! Karen had asked me to speak at her church women's conference for the second consecutive year. The conference the year before had been such a special time for the women and for me, a high holy worship day in which the Lord healed and delivered.

As I prepared for the upcoming conference, I studied my Bible, took copious notes, and organized in my mind what I wanted to say and how I wanted to express it. I completed all my research and studied and defined every word I had questions about. I did everything I could think of to make this message even better than last year's. But something was missing.

The day came; the hour for speaking was nearly upon me. Even though I had studied, prepared, and rehearsed in my mind, something was still missing. Before I spoke, I asked my assistant, Pat, to pray for me because I was so unsettled. She, too, sensed that something was not right. But even her righteous prayers did not settle my spirit.

I went ahead and spoke, God moved, and people were helped. In the middle of my speech, the Holy Spirit turned the course of what I was saying into a personal testimony about my marriage. Women throughout the sanctuary were moved to tears. God clearly was in control. But something was still missing.

All the compliments and accolades I received after the message did not assuage my discomfort. The women who shared lunch with me after I spoke told me how powerful my message had been. But my spirit remained troubled.

Later that evening, I got on my knees at home and said, "Okay, God. You moved today in spite of me. But what was missing? Did I do what you wanted me to? People were helped. Marriages were saved. But I feel so very far from you. What's wrong?"

I waited on his answer, and it came to me as clear as day: "You never asked me what *I* wanted you to say. You just went out on your own without consulting me!"

The truth hit me like the proverbial ton of bricks. He was right! Not once in the course of preparing for the message did I ask God for his guidance. I simply considered the theme requested by Karen and based what I was going to say on what she said she wanted, not on what God wanted. Only after I asked for wisdom from God and took time to listen did he reveal to me what had been missing all along. After I repented, he sent a portion of peace my way.

I've always made a habit of asking for God's guidance. So what happened this time? For that, I don't have a good answer. Perhaps I got so caught up in the events of the week and the deadlines that I simply forgot who's in charge. I'm not — that's for sure! It could be that my ego was on the front burner because I wanted to surpass last year's "performance." I honestly don't know what I was thinking about instead of my Master.

God could have gotten very angry with me and decided to show me up in front of all those people by allowing me to fall flat on my face. But he didn't. My neglecting him did not deter him from doing what he wanted to do for the women at that conference. He completely revised my speech and caused words to flow from my mouth that I had never even considered saying to that crowd. Even though I had not asked for his advice, God did take control. He made good what could have ended badly.

It's amazing to me how, in spite of our natural neglect of God, he uses us for his glory. He shows up with his extravagant grace, grants us undeserved favor, and allows us to carry out what he has started.

Have you ever known in your "knower" that something was wrong, but you could not put your finger on the problem? Learn from my mistake. Ask for wisdom. If you don't hear from God immediately, pray for seven days that he will speak to you. Seven is said to be the number of completion. If you ask God sincerely in faith, believing he will answer you, he will not disappoint you.

I had to learn the hard way: "When you ask, you do not receive, because you ask with wrong motives, that you may spend what you get on your pleasures" (James 4:3). Now I make it a practice to remind myself of the liberating truth: "Thelma, trust in the LORD with all your heart and lean not on your own understanding; in all your ways acknowledge him, and he will make your paths straight" (Proverbs 3:5–6). Now that's grace!

If any of you lacks wisdom, he should ask God,
who gives generously to all without finding fault,
and it will be given to him.

JAMES 1:5

❧

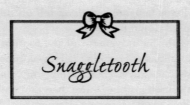

Snaggletooth

LUCI SWINDOLL

๑

*When we understand that God has called us individually
by name, it profoundly alters the way we live.*

MOTHER ANGELICA

One of my favorite television commercials has no
words. A young woman walks into a shop and
admires a bathing suit on a mannequin. With a look of
self-satisfaction, she picks up a suit like it, disappears into
a dressing room, throws her own clothes over the door,
then, after a couple seconds, lets out a blood-curdling
scream. It's a powerhouse endorsement of the diet the
commercial recommends. I laugh every time I see it as I
munch away on my Snickers.

How many times do we look in the mirror and find no
words to express what we see? The mirror talks. We
scream. Thelma has a good idea. She says, "I'm fully
clothed when I look in the mirror 'cause I don't want
nuthin' talkin' back to me." Well put!

Recently I had a little screaming fit in front of my
bathroom mirror. The dentist had attached a temporary
cap on one of my permanent front teeth, which he had
earlier filed away to a tiny squared-off yellow stub. That

night when I was brushing, the cap fell off into the sink and disappeared down the drain.

At first, with the movement of the toothbrush and a mouthful of toothpaste, I couldn't tell it was gone. I just had a virtual sense of vacancy. Then, running my tongue across my front teeth, I felt nothing more than that stub. The cap was gone. For good. Forever. Forsooth! (Actually, I thought something else, but you don't want to know.)

I smiled into the mirror, then screamed. In short, I panicked. And I rarely panic. Generally I'm very calm, and little makes me lose my cool. But losing my tooth? Well, I lost my cool. I moaned, groaned, whimpered, and wailed. (It's hard to do all that at the same time, but I managed.) I looked in the mirror, hoping a second glance might bring back the tooth, but saw only that awful, gaping hole.

While pacing the hallway, I asked the Lord to take my life. I prayed for the return of Christ. This gaping hole in my mouth was a serious problem. I was leaving at dawn the next morning for Cincinnati.

With an unsteady hand I eventually dialed my dentist at home, told him I had to speak to 15,000 women at a conference the next day, and had no front tooth. I just knew he'd say, "Oh, honey, I understand. You come to the office right now and I'll fix everything." But he didn't. He promised to meet me the next morning before my flight.

The next *morning?* He might as well have said in my next lifetime! Needless to say, I had a restless night envisioning the most embarrassing moment of my life surrounded by a sea of laughing women.

The next day Dr. Baumann and I both showed up early and the replacement was done. A very caring, kind man, he looked at me and said (with both fists and several tons of metal in my mouth), "Luci . . . what if you had to speak with that stub showing? You're still the same person inside, aren't you?"

That'th eathy for you to thay, pal. But, you know what? It's true. No matter how different I look on the outside, I'm still me behind that snaggletooth. And I'll be me when I'm completely toothless one day! God, have mercy.

Sometimes the hardest thing in life is being ourselves. We so want to be somebody else. For years I sang with the Dallas Opera chorus, playing the part of other people. It was great. I wore wigs, corsets, fake eyelashes, heavy makeup, and costumes in order to become a waitress or a factory worker, a nun, courtesan, schoolteacher, soldier, witch, dancer, or lady-in-waiting. Whatever was called for, I became that. Interestingly, even my friends in the chorus used to say, "My favorite thing about all this is that I don't have to be me."

The next time you stand in front of a mirror and want to scream, try to remember that God made that face. That smile. Those big eyes, crooked teeth, and chubby cheeks. You are his creation, called to reflect him. Spiritual transformation doesn't come from a diet program, a bottle, a makeover, or mask. It comes from an intimate relationship with the Savior. Because of his gracious nature, he looks beyond our snaggletoothed grin and appreciates us for who we really are. So we can, too.

> *The LORD does not look at the things man looks at. Man looks at the outward appearance, but the LORD looks at the heart.*
>
> 1 SAMUEL 16:7

Power in the Blood

MARILYN MEBERG

❧

*God does what we cannot do so we can be
what we dare not dream: perfect before God.*

MAX LUCADO

I don't like all this blood talk! Why can't you Christians just talk about God's love? That's much more appealing."

The woman who made this statement wasn't being critical or unpleasant ... she simply found the "blood talk," in a word, "disgusting." She also told me that she's never understood why Jesus had to die. Why was it necessary? Why couldn't God just love his creation without making it so bloody messy?

Most of us who have been raised in Christian traditions have perhaps gotten used to phrases like "all things are cleansed with blood" and that "without the shedding of blood there is no forgiveness" (Hebrews 9:22). More challenging to our sensibilities perhaps are the words in John 6:54: "Whoever eats my flesh and drinks my blood has eternal life." Now there's a verse that probably would drive the woman bothered by "blood talk" to the first exit at a fast trot! We, of course, know that it refers to the sacrament of Communion, but to someone not schooled in the Scriptures, it could sound like an invitation for vampires.

Don't you think it's interesting that the medical world talks about blood all the time and no one would think of accusing them of being obsessive about it. The medical world *is* obsessed with blood, and I'm so glad it is. With the emergence of HIV and Hepatitis C, it is frightening to consider the possibility of getting tainted blood in the event that a need for a transfusion should arise. If someone is cut or injured severely, the first concern doctors have is that the person not bleed to death. Blood is an absolute necessity. Without it we die. As Leviticus 17:11 states, "the life of a creature is in the blood."

In the Old Testament, God set forth for his people an elaborate system of sacrificing animals as a way to get forgiveness for sin. In God's justice system, the consequences of a person's sin was death, so an animal was killed as a symbolic way to pay the penalty for that sin. And not just any animal could be chosen. It had to be perfect. It couldn't be sick, have any blemishes, be missing a leg, or prone to seizures. As the animal was sacrificed, the people would confess their sin in an effort to make peace with God.

When Jesus came to earth, his whole purpose was to become the ultimate sacrifice for the human sins that required the death penalty. No longer would goats or sheep be sacrificed; he himself, the perfect Son of God, would die for sinners! Only Jesus, who knew no sin, who was utterly perfect, qualified as the sacrifice that was acceptable to God. He, instead of an animal, shed his blood for the sins of the world.

He also bypassed the sacrifices consisting of goat and calf blood, instead using his own blood as

the price to set us free once and for all. If that animal blood and the other rituals of purification were
effective in cleaning up certain matters of our reli-
gion and behavior, think how much more the blood
of Christ cleans up our whole lives, inside and out.
(Hebrews 9, THE MESSAGE)

Now what does all this have to do with grace? It was
the gracious love of God that sent the perfect sacrifice to
die for the sins of the world. That gracious act not only
secures my eternal salvation but also assures me of God's
grace for life. Because of what Jesus did for me I need
never worry about being separated from God's presence.
He cleansed me from all sin and sees me as perfect,
cleansed by the blood of his righteous Son. Mind bog-
gling!

Crawl into the assurance of Romans 8:1 and let it
wrap around you like a down comforter.

With the arrival of Jesus, the Messiah, that
fateful dilemma is resolved. Those who enter into
Christ's being-there-for-us no longer have to live
under a continuous, low-lying black cloud. A
new power is in operation. The Spirit of life in
Christ, like a strong wind, has magnificently
cleared the air, freeing you from a fated lifetime
of brutal tyranny at the hands of sin and death.
(THE MESSAGE)

All this because of the shed blood of Jesus!
I can understand why those who don't recognize the
power in Christ's blood would find all the "blood talk" a
bit unsavory, to say the least. But to those of us who have
been washed in that blood, it is the greatest gift of all.

*For what the law was powerless to do in
that it was weakened by the sinful nature,
God did by sending his own Son in the likeness
of sinful man to be a sin offering.*

ROMANS 8:3

~

Say Thank You

SHEILA WALSH

Were there no God we would be in this glorious world with grateful hearts and no one to thank.

CHRISTINA ROSSETTI

I'm learning to stop for thankful moments. It's become a daily discipline of mine since I found that I was getting overwhelmed by all the daily stuff that "has to get done." Some of the feelings and fears I had before I was hospitalized for clinical depression were niggling at me again, buzzing around me like persistent house flies. I've learned enough about what makes me tick to pay attention when I feel myself sinking. So I'm learning to stop intentionally throughout every day and lift my heart and soul to heaven and say, "Thank you!"

Giving thanks does wonders for my soul. It refocuses me on what's really important so that instead of dwelling on the fact that Christian just tried to flush my new pale blue suede pumps down the toilet, I can celebrate the gift of a child when so many arms are empty. Marcus Aurelius, a first-century Roman emperor, wrote that the most important thing a man can choose is how he thinks. We can dwell every day on the things that are not working and let them drag us down, or we can thank God for the simple gifts of grace he gives us every day if we have a heart to see them.

When Barry's mom's liver cancer had spread to the degree that she was receiving in-home hospice care, she told me about the many people who dropped by every day to say "hi" or to bring some crab soup to try to tempt her to eat. "Sometimes you don't stop to think how many good friends you have until a time like this," Eleanor said.

That thought sat on my shoulder like a small bird waiting to be fed. One March evening when we were visiting Eleanor in Charleston, Barry and I went out for a drive through the beautiful countryside. Suddenly the idea occurred to me: "Here's what I'd like to do," I said. "We'll have a good photo taken of you and Christian and me and get it enlarged, then cut it into pieces."

Barry looked at me as if the strain of his mom's illness had pushed me off a mental bridge. "Like a jigsaw puzzle," I explained. "We'll send a piece of the puzzle to each of our dear friends with a letter telling them why we're grateful to them, what they add to our lives, and how God has used them to fill in the missing pieces in our hearts. Then at Christmastime we'll invite them to a party at our house. We'll ask them to bring their piece, and we'll give them a gift specially chosen to highlight what they mean to us."

Barry was still looking at me as if I needed more sleep. I pressed on as we women have to when they don't get it.

"At the end of the evening we'll glue all the pieces back together, a visual picture of how our friends have added to our lives and how truly grateful we are for each one of them."

"What made you think of that?" Barry asked as we drove across the river.

"Don't you think it's a good idea?" I asked him.

"Sure I do," he replied, "but what made you think of it?"

"I don't really know. Sometimes I just want to find more ways to say thank you."

"So you just thought of that?" Barry pressed.

"Yes!"

"And you're feeling all right?"

"Yes!"

I smiled. "It's like what we're trying to teach Christian. We tell him it's not enough just to say 'Sorry' when he does something wrong. Instead we ask him to tell us what he's sorry for. So perhaps it's not always enough to say 'Thanks,' either. We need to say what we're thankful for."

As I lay in bed that night after swallowing the two aspirin Barry gave me, I thought about how the same principle applies to our relationship with God. Instead of just tossing off a "Hey, thanks!" now and then as we hustle through life, why not make it a practice to thank him very specifically for his goodness to us?

In her book *Basket of Blessings: 31 Days to a More Grateful Heart*, Karen O'Connor shares her experience with just such a practice. "If you want to be content, to experience peace," a friend had told Karen, "write down your blessings — the things you're grateful for — on slips of paper and put them in a container of some kind. A small basket or box or bag will do. Soon it will be full to overflowing. From time to time look at what you wrote. No one can be discontent for long with so much to be thankful for."

In addition to filling a "blessing basket" on a daily basis, we could write a letter to God once a year, listing all that pours out of our hearts for his extravagant grace to us. Think of what a joy it would be to keep our annual letters of gratitude to read through the years or to pass on to our children.

Whether our "thank you's" are momentary, intentional pauses in the midst of a hectic day, thank-you notes to God for his many blessings, or lengthy discourses of his grace, cultivating an attitude of gratitude will remind us of the truth that undergirds our lives: "For the LORD is good and his love endures forever; his faithfulness continues through all generations" (Psalm 100:5).

> *Enter his gates with thanksgiving and*
> *his courts with praise; give thanks*
> *to him and praise his name.*
>
> PSALM 100:4

❧

Enjoying
the Gift

Hound Haven B&B

PATSY CLAIRMONT

❧

What is sacred delight? A day's wage paid to workers who had worked only one hour ... the father scrubbing the pig smell off his son's back ... the shepherd throwing a party because the sheep was found.

MAX LUCADO

My friend Janet must have a dog-bone-shaped B&B sign hanging over her porch that only hounds can detect. Every lost little lamb of a dog that wanders through the neighborhood gravitates to her home. Be they small, tall, chunky, or lean, these persistent pets (of others) line up for their turn to lap up her grace-filled hospitality.

In the three years she's lived at this house, Janet has entertained everything from huskies who took her for walks, cockapoos who slept quietly at her feet while she worked, a corgi named Corkie, and the prerequisite mutts. Sometimes when the winds are fierce and fences are blown down, dogs, unexposed to the wonders of wandering, meander on over to Hound Haven. Puck the Airedale loves to regularly jaunt up the street on a lark, having devised perpetually new and creative ways to escape his fenced yard several blocks away. He has become a regular boarder.

Usually the visiting canines wear name tags replete with the dog's name, owner's name, address, and phone number. When these dogs are discovered, Janet phones the owner (who is never home) and leaves a message reporting the whereabouts of Teddy, Puck, or Milton. Then the dogs settle in for the day. Between six and seven in the evening, the owner invariably calls, and a happy reunion takes place after a dog day of scarfing up snacks, begging for more ear-rubbing, and enjoying deliciously long naps.

All generally goes well for these wayward dogs, and they're content to live in the luxury of Hound Haven — until four in the afternoon. Without fail, each dog seems to sense all is not right with the world at teatime. They awaken from a day of slumber to whine. Or they become restless and demand to go outside, where they whine. Or they plant their heads in Janet's lap and whine. Then both dog and B&B owner long for the pet to be quickly restored to his rightful owner.

Each day when Janet opens her door, she never knows what she might find, or should I say whom. But one thing is certain: Word has spread that this is the place for grace, where wandering souls will find someone who will lovingly care for them. At Hound Haven, dogs can simply be — and bask in a kind woman's delight.

Janet's tender care of other people's pets reflects how God takes sacred delight in heaping grace on wayward beings. He actually enjoys scrubbing the pig smell off the son who has come home. God relishes throwing a party for the lost lamb who has been found. And he revels in the moment we return to him from our spiritual wanderings.

I can just imagine him smiling in delight as he enfolds us in his arms and whispers, "Welcome home, little one." Why, it's enough to make one's tail wag just thinking about it.

You were like sheep going astray,
but now you have returned to the Shepherd
and Overseer of your souls.

1 PETER 2:25

❧

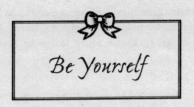

Be Yourself

THELMA WELLS

*God has a purpose for each one of us, a work for
each one to do, an influence for each one to exert,
a likeness to His dear Son for each one to manifest, and
then a place for each one to fill in His holy temple.*

ARTHUR C. A. HALL

*W*hat comes to mind when you think of the word
authority?

Webster's defines authority as a noun: "The power or
right to command, act . . ."

But what does authority mean to a child of God?

The word *authority* has a word in it that tells the whole
story: "author." Author means creator, organizer, cause,
source of things. Authority is what you are authorized to do.
It is the work to which you are called by God, who is the
author and finisher of your faith. As a child of God, your
authority is determined by God, and your authenticity is
determined by how you fulfill what God has entrusted to
you. Your authority is your calling, appointment, ordination,
assignment, gifts, talents, and personal passion given to you
by God to be carried out for his purposes. Wow!

In light of the spiritual meaning of authority, consider this: When we try to do and act like other people, we are acting in an unauthorized capacity. When we try to be someone we're not, when we try to emulate gifts, skills, and characteristics that are not ours, we abuse the authority we have been given as individuals whom God has blessed with a unique purpose.

I have the God-given authority to speak convincingly, powerfully, and boldly for the Lord. If I had the opportunity, I would get up every morning and speak somewhere. That's my passion in life. God called me to do that and continually gives me everything it takes to speak — the knowledge, the engagements, and the words to say. I love it so much that I give away a lot of time, effort, energy, and experience doing what I'm called to do without getting overly tired.

There are some things, however, that I cannot do well. I've tried, but it just doesn't work. For example, I took piano lessons for four years, trying to learn to play like one of my best friends. During that period of time, I told her how angry and frustrated I was because I was not able to play a piano like she can. In fact, I could not play a piano like *anyone* who can play. For three years I agonized over my inability to get out of Thompson's Book One. You know, the red book. For hours I would sit at my piano and attempt to make music. Instead, noise came out of it. I rationalized that it was the piano that sounded so bad, so I sold that old piano and bought a new namebrand job. Believe me, it was not the piano.

Sometimes I became so frustrated that I would literally sit at the piano and cry. One day, in the midst of my pity party, the light came on: "Thelma, why don't you ask your friend to play for you while you sing. She can play, you can't. You can sing, she can't."

What a brilliant idea! Sometimes I'm slow. It took me three years to figure out that I'd been agonizing and fretting over something that I had absolutely no "authority" over or in! God did not call me to play a piano, he called me to sing and to speak and to bear witness to his grace. I started realizing that when I'd sung at church throughout my life, entered oratorical contests all through school, and always jumped at the chance to be in front of an audience even as a little girl, God was preparing me to fulfill my "authority." My college preparation to be a teacher and my years teaching children and adults honed my God-given skills for the day when I would start my own speaking business and later speak before thousands of people in conferences all over the world.

Honey, if you are trying to be something you know you aren't, if you are trying to do things you know you have little ability, patience, passion, commitment, and tolerance for, cut it out! Be yourself! The great thing about real authority is that God gives me one thing to do, somebody else another, somebody else something else; or he may give us the same talent but have us exhibit it in different ways. Blending our authority with other people's authority creates the kind of kingdom on earth that personifies God's kingdom in heaven. The reason Lucifer was kicked out of heaven was that he tried to usurp God's authority and be something he wasn't. How very stupid when he had the fourth best position in heaven! His jealousy and rebellion cost him his position, his beauty, his ability to make angelic music, and his intimacy with God. When we operate outside of our authority, we experience similar breakdowns.

But that doesn't have to happen to you. Just be who you are, what you are, how you are, the way God made you. It is his grace that creates in you the talents, inclinations, knowledge, and *pleasure* to be yourself. Grace empowers you to perform the tasks God has given you on earth, and to enjoy what he has called you to do. And, Baby, it's all just a rehearsal for when we will rule and reign with him on high!

Now the body is not made up of one part but of many. . . . If the whole body were an eye, where would the sense of hearing be? If the whole body were an ear, where would the sense of smell be? But in fact God has arranged the parts in the body, every one of them, just as he wanted them to be.

1 Corinthians 12:14, 17–18

~

God's E-mail

BARBARA JOHNSON

❧

I am in complete control. It's the situation that is out of hand.

A little girl was learning the Lord's Prayer. Each night at bedtime her mother carefully repeated it. At last the child was ready to try it on her own. She knelt down, folded her hands, and began to pray. Each line was perfect until: "... and lead us not into temptation ... but deliver us some e-mail."

God chuckles at our innocent mistakes. And he proclaims truth through children, because God does deliver e-mail — just when we need it most! The King of kings gives you and me access into his grace over the phone line of faith — direct to his royal chat room. His e-mail address is Jeremiah33:3@don'tstress.com: "Call to me and I will answer you and tell you great and unsearchable things you do not know."

Some of us are technologically challenged. I understand that. It can be intimidating to get into a brand new mode of communication when you're used to old-fashioned tools like telephones, typewriters, or even fountain pens. Once I sat down at a computer to log onto the Internet. The screen directed me to "PRESS ANY

KEY." I looked all over for the "ANY" key and couldn't find it!

I put my disk into the slot. Nothing appeared on the screen, so I called Computerland for help. The service department told me to put my disk back into the slot and be sure to close the door. I told the customer service guy to hold on. When I got up and closed the door to my office, the disk still didn't work. The screen scoffed at me, chiding "bad command," and called me "invalid." The service man said I shouldn't take it personally. But what was I to think? (Life was so much easier when it was just Dick, Jane, and Spot, wasn't it?) That afternoon, I went back to my dependable typewriter. My writing flowed. Now that is grace!

I am thankful that even when I don't understand the Lord or his ways (just like I don't understand the Internet), I can still depend on him by faith. When computers, calendars, and clocks seem to get the best of me and my time, I rely on the One who never changes. I figure God put me on earth to accomplish a certain number of things (right now I'm so far behind, I'll never die), but God is my hiding place from the tyranny of the urgent. Because of his grace, I can luxuriate in knowledge that all is well — even when the bits and bytes of my life look like scrambled gobbledygook.

The apostle Paul reminds us that through Christ, "we have gained access by faith into this grace in which we now stand" (Romans 5:2). Like the Internet superhighway, we have access to grace at any time of day or night. This grace connects us with God himself and with people worldwide who have signed on to follow him. By faith we hyperlink to the wisdom we need to live by his kingdom principles. His extravagant grace is available in a fraction of the time it takes to go through the red tape of the Department of Human Services.

What is it you need today? Remember that you have immediate access to God's Riches At Christ's Expense (GRACE). It's all right there, waiting for you to dial in. Jesus said, "God's kingdom is within you." Click on that!

> *We throw open our doors to God and discover*
> *at the same moment that he has already thrown*
> *open his door to us. We find ourselves standing*
> *where we always hoped we might stand—*
> *out in the wide open spaces of God's grace and*
> *glory, standing tall and shouting our praise.*

ROMANS 5:2–3 (THE MESSAGE)

❧

A Little Whine with Your Cheese?

PATSY CLAIRMONT

❧

Grace, indeed, is beauty in action.
DISRAELI

Sick takes grace. No, let me restate that. Doing sick well takes grace. I personally don't do sick well. I whine well. (Everyone has her strengths.) Actually, I excel in the art of whining.

I learned to whine as the baby girl in our family line. That is, until I was thirteen, and then my sister was born, and I had to grow up . . . a little. After thirteen years of whining, though, I had established a response pattern that was hard to shake. Ask my husband. No, on second thought, don't.

To whine well you must learn to make your words singsong to the tune of, say, a dirge. Then you must drag out your syllables: "I don't waan-nahhh." You may want to practice that. Emphasis and drama play key roles in the act of being truly nauseating. Body language is also important to convey an all-over whine: Shoulders should slump forward, head should wag, and whatever you do, don't forget the lip. The bottom one must protrude about three inches, heading south toward your shuffling feet.

Are you getting the picture? Pretty, huh? After you've mastered the art, plan on spending a lot of time alone.

Oh, did I fail to mention that one of the side effects of being a whiner is people tire of you pronto? That response gives the whiner something new to — what else — whine about. So if you're going to be a serious whiner, it will help if you like the sound of your own voice.

By the way, the higher your voice's octave, the more annoying it will be to others. That can be temporarily effective, but I must warn you that long term it may decrease your life expectancy. Folks can be so intolerant.

Of course, "silent whining" is also very effective. The silence screams, "Look at me, notice me, fix my unhappiness!" This type of whiner is able to manage entire households without a word. Often you'll find her sitting in her room alone for days, waiting to be rescued by some guilt-ridden relative. Such whiners gravitate toward rocking chairs. The type with squeaks are the most appealing so the whiner can send a cranky lullaby throughout the dwelling. Voiceless whiners are the ones who slam cupboards and doors to make a point and then, when confronted, swear that nothing is bothering them.

Grace has a very different look (whew). Soft like down, gentle like a summer breeze. Its sound is a rippling brook, a sparrow's song, a hymn of praise. Grace wears well. It is chiffon, it is silk, it is gossamer. Others welcome grace, like a sister, a friend, a Savior. Grace moves with the ease of a monarch butterfly and the lilt of a leaf pirouetting toward the earth. Grace curtsies. Grace is polite, spacious, and richly endowed. Grace bows to serve and reigns with mercy.

Whiners neither enjoy nor give joy. But grace-filled people are reputable, sought after, and deeply loved. They stand heads above others even while on their knees. They are full of forgiveness and wisdom. You often find them nurturing children, caring for the ill, serving the under-privileged, applauding the successes of others, and cele-brating God's generosity.

Grace is Ruth of the Bible, bent over in the scorching fields to feed herself and her mother-in-law. Grace is Naomi embracing Ruth's baby as if it were her own. Grace is Abigail, facedown in the dirt before David as an advocate for her workers. It is Esther, kneeling before the king on behalf of a nation. It is Hagar, returning submis-sively to her angered employer. It is Hannah, turning her young son Samuel over to the priest Eli, as she promised. Grace is a young virgin who cried, "Be it unto me accord-ing to thy word" (Luke 1:38 KJV).

Yes, grace knows how to suffer well . . . and how to live well. Do we?

> *All beautiful you are, my darling;*
> *there is no flaw in you.*
> SONG OF SONGS 4:7

⮞

My Backyard Sanctuary

LUCI SWINDOLL

❦

With God's enablement live this day to the full—
as if it were your last day on earth.

CHUCK SWINDOLL

For six months the plants on my patio have been either dead or dying. I've heard their little throats rattle each time I walk outside. Having had my fill of this I decided, two weeks ago, to spend whatever time it took to bring new life to the patio.

I went to the nursery, bought luxuriant flowering plants, potting soil, and pony packs. Four days, two blistered hands, and one achy-breaky back later, I have something akin to Monet's garden at Giverny — though on a smaller scale. I even bought a new patio chair and table so I could enjoy my garden in the cool of the evenings. It is one spiffy spot and brings pure pleasure and sheer satisfaction. Every day I deadhead plants, encouraging each plant to blossom anew by removing the old, faded flowers. I water, study growth, visit with the little blossoms, and cut bouquets for the house. That's what I was doing this morning when I heard a whooshing sound.

Looking up, I saw right over my head a huge, colorful hot-air balloon. Oh. My. Gosh. For a minute I thought it might land on the patio. I ran in, grabbed my camera, and was back in a flash, taking pictures. Somebody from the basket yelled down, "Good morning!" *Well, I guess!* Then more balloons came. And more. In all, there were a dozen filling the sky. My own private show. Nobody was out there to see them but my trusty little camera and me. I shot a whole roll of film, just like that. And it all happened before 7 A.M. What a way to start a day.

When was the last time you walked outside and looked around? Or up? Or under? Or through the leaves and limbs of a tree to see what was there? There's something, I can tell you for sure. It's waiting to be discovered and enjoyed — by you.

The backyard of the house where I used to live is a perfect example. It had an enormous spreading sycamore tree with branches reaching into the next county. A majestic, hovering thing! I was standing under it one day talking with a friend when she said quietly, "Turn around very slowly, Luci. Look up in the tree. On a low branch is a huge horned owl." Neither of us could believe our eyes. We stared. He stared back, unblinking. What a magnificent moment. Keeping my eyes on the owl, I whispered, "Whatever you do, honey, don't let that owl leave before I get a picture. I'll be right back."

Because I keep my camera loaded with film and just inside the doorway, I was able to snatch it and get several good shots before the owl moved, blinked, or thought twice. Actually, he stayed there most of the day, claiming that branch for himself. He was a wise old bird who knew what he wanted. I named him Wizard. It became almost a daily routine for me to watch for Wizard with my binoculars out my bedroom window.

One morning about 7:45, a fascinating drama unfolded in that tree. A red-shouldered hawk decided he wanted Wizard's spot and swooped down with lots of "kyaah, kyaah, kyaahs." Joining this audible fray were black grackles, mockingbirds, and a pair of out-numbered house wrens. I'd never heard such a racket. It went on for five or ten minutes and I witnessed the whole thing from my window. That night in my journal I recorded it, with drawings of the birds and the tree. It was September 18, 1993.

Then two months later something entirely different but equally as fascinating happened. My journal entry:

> You're not going to believe this, Journal, but I was opening my bedroom shutters this morning at 6:30 on a dark, rainy day ... it was just dawn ... and I saw a big dog (without a leash) on my back grassy knoll. It was loping or kind of stalking. Strange looking. Big tail. Suddenly, I realized it was a coyote. I watched it with my binoculars until it finally wandered off down by Gestapo's house.

("Gestapo" is the name I gave the neighborhood creep. He patrolled the out-of-doors — never finding anything pleasurable as far as I know.)

Check out your own backyard. Keep your eyes peeled. God's gracious gifts are everywhere ... wrapped in a bird's nest, or popping out of the ground, or flying overhead. Take a picture. Write it down. Make a drawing. Enjoy!

Give thanks to the LORD for his
unfailing love and his wonderful deeds.

PSALM 107:8

❧

Quackers

MARILYN MEBERG

❦

*The cross means that intimacy with God is wildly,
wonderfully possible.*

TIMOTHY JONES

I love out-of-the-norm experiences that feed the
quirky side of my soul. So when I found out that an
upcoming Women of Faith conference was to be held in
Memphis, Tennessee, and we'd be staying at the Peabody
Hotel, I was delighted.

You see, the Peabody is home to a little flock of ducks
that put on a show each day for an audience of hotel
guests who apparently have nothing better to do than to
set their watches by Duck Time. Just before eleven
o'clock each morning, a red carpet is laid out from the elevator to the marble fountain in the middle of the hotel
lobby. At exactly eleven, the elevator doors burst open
and five ducks dash through them, race down the carpet
at top speed, and then pitch headfirst into the fountain
water. They swim around in there all day until the red carpet is once again stretched out at five o'clock. They wad-
dle back down the carpet into the elevator where they're
whisked up to their little duck penthouse for the night.

Once there, I envision them snacking on duck pate (ducks have no loyalty . . . the pate is probably the bird that moved too slowly) and quacking about the day's performance.

Seeing the feathered little ruffians' escapades for myself gave me an enormous giggle. In talking briefly with one of the hotel personnel, I commented on the speed and energy with which the ducks exited the elevator in their pell-mell race for the fountain. He told me I'd probably burst through the doors too if I had a trainer with a little stick behind my back. Being assured that the ducks were well-treated and the stick was only a symbol of rarely used encouragement, I threaded my way through the people-jammed lobby to the gift shop where I belonged.

Oddly enough, though, the image of the ducks with a stick poised at their backs to ensure good performance stuck with me. How grateful I am that God doesn't use such means to keep me in line! Instead, he extends a luxurious grace that allows me to stay on the elevator if I want to — or sprawl out on the red carpet until day's end. God's grace is about no performance and no stick.

In fact, grace is about a loving father who not only does not demand performance but he seeks to support us in what we do. Second Chronicles 16:9 assures us: "For the eyes of the LORD move to and fro throughout the earth that He may strongly support those whose heart is completely His" (NASB).

What a fantastic image! God searching, watching, seeking us out wherever we are on the earth. And for what purpose? That he might give us support! Support . . . not condemnation. Support . . . not criticism. Support . . . not rejection. God searches for us not to wield a stick but to offer encouragement.

There are those believers for whom that message of grace does not compute. It defies logic; it can't really be true; and certainly it can't be meant for the likes of us. Those are the people we see day in and day out, living their lives with a sense of frantic urgency, afraid that at any moment they're going to feel the stick. But God says to them: "Come to Me all you who are weary and heavy laden, and I will give you rest" (Matthew 11:28 NASB).

Where there is grace there is no stick. Instead there is rest . . . and sweet support.

> *Before this faith came, we were held prisoners*
> *by the law, locked up until faith should be*
> *revealed. So the law was put in charge to*
> *lead us to Christ that we might be justified*
> *by faith. Now that faith has come,*
> *we are no longer under the supervision*
> *of the law.*
>
> GALATIANS 3:23–25

❧

Haulin' Freedom

LUCI SWINDOLL

❧

*Every place has its pitfalls and absurdities,
just as each has its opportunities and measures of grace.*
DANIEL TAYLOR

*I*f there ever was a place that lends itself to one's expression of autonomy, it's the Los Angeles freeway system. I don't know if it's because so many of the freeways lead to Hollywood and folks think there might be a talent scout in their lane looking for the next Thelma and Louise, or because O. J. Simpson gained such notoriety racing north on the 405 in search of his own freedom. There's just something about the word *freeway* that makes people think it's exactly that: their way to freedom.

During my twenty-five years in California, I've seen it all: Daredevil pedestrians running across the freeway at rush hour. Some poor soul trying to jump off an overpass. Motorcyclists weaving at breakneck speed between moving vehicles. Two motorists parked on the shoulder throwing rocks at one another's cars. I've witnessed creative hand gestures, men shaving, women applying mascara, violent arguments, speed races, road rage, romance, and other acts of recklessness. (Did I ever tell you about the time I saw a clown in the driver's seat?)

Undoubtedly, the most ingenious expression of "freeway freedom" I ever saw was on a summer afternoon. I don't remember the temperature, but it was hot and getting hotter! Nobody wants to be anywhere on a day like that, much less in traffic. It was ghastly.

There I was, driving along, when suddenly out of my peripheral vision I spotted something I could not believe. In the middle lane was a pickup truck, going about 50 mph, with a makeshift swimming pool rigged up in the bed of the truck. Three children were having the time of their lives, yelling, splashing water, diving in, horsing around with rubber toys. I will have to say it looked so inviting I considered joining them. I didn't, of course, but I did join all the other motorists in my lane as we created what we refer to in California as "gawker's block" — slow down and stare.

The driver of this moving circus animatedly chatted with his passenger in the cab as they raced blithely along. Music was blasting out the windows, and everybody was happy as a clam. The driver was oblivious to the stir he was causing, and certainly was unaware he was about to be in a heap of trouble for endangering the lives of those in his pickup!

It wasn't until the next morning when I opened the newspaper that I learned what finally happened. There was a photo of this very truck, wet children, and embarrassed driver as a police officer was handing him a traffic citation for breaking the law. The short article quoted the driver as saying, "It was so hot and the kids were having so much fun, I just hated to stop them."

Everybody in that truck thought they were free to do whatever they wanted — if they were thinking at all. Their perspective reminded me of the line Debbie Boone sings in "You Light Up My Life": "How can it be wrong when it feels so right?" Haven't we all thought that at times? During the sixties, there was strong emphasis on expressing your freedom no matter what: let your hair grow, burn your bra and your draft card, sleep in the grass, make love not war, cry freedom — from parental rule, regimentation, traditions, the control of others. And yet, is this really freedom?

Well, this I know: Freedom is not taking the law into our own hands. It's not putting someone else at risk. It's not doing what we please simply because it feels "good" or "right." If we want to truly enjoy freedom, we need to realize that our liberty was bought at an exorbitant price and carries with it an enormous responsibility. It's based on grace, found in the life, death, and resurrection of Jesus Christ. And it's expressed in service, not sanction. In giving, not getting. In liberty, not license. It's not doing what we please, it's pleasing God in what we do. That's where real freedom lies.

The book of Galatians teaches that we've been set free to serve the Savior joyfully, not the law grudgingly. Our greatest way to freedom is obeying and serving Jesus Christ. Now, that's a truth worth haulin' down the freeway.

Don't you know that when you offer yourselves to someone to obey him as slaves, you are slaves to the one whom you obey—whether you are slaves to sin, which leads to death, or to obedience, which leads to righteousness?

ROMANS 6:16

∞

Sundays with Edna

LUCI SWINDOLL

❧

When grace is joined with wrinkles, it is adorable.
There is an unspeakable dawn in happy old age.

VICTOR HUGO

Even though (according to Abigail Van Buren) folks are worth a fortune in old age "with silver in their hair, gold in their teeth, stones in their kidneys, lead in their feet and gas in their stomachs," aging is a journey we don't eagerly anticipate. As Henry James says, it's like walking into "enemy territory." Who knows what we'll encounter on the road ahead? Loneliness, wrinkles, stiff joints, indigestion, memory loss? We envision lugging a suitcase full of pills instead of party dresses, and trying to jump-start a mind that operates on only two cylinders, if and when it goes into gear.

My friend Edna defied all those stereotypes of "old." When we met, I was twenty and she was eighty. She lived alone in a three-room house two blocks from the college campus where I was a student. One of my greatest delights that year was visiting Edna. Her daughter, Marian, and I sang together in the church choir. One Sunday after the service, she invited a group of students to lunch, then to her mother's home. The idea of eating at the City Café held much more appeal than dorm dining, so there was a resounding *yes* from all of us. I thought the meal would be the highlight of that invitation, but I was wrong. It was Edna, the youngest old person I've ever known.

When we approached the little clapboard house in which Edna lived, I loved it immediately. There were flowers in abundance — all over the yard as well as in window boxes at every window. Classical music filled the air, along with the aroma of fresh baking bread. I wanted to take in everything as quickly as possible for fear it would be over too soon.

Edna, a sprightly, animated little woman, greeted Marian warmly, and when she was introduced to each of us, she curtsied and smiled. "Welcome to my house . . . how about a cup of tea?" I could hardly believe my eyes . . . ears . . . nose. Humming along with the music, Edna went into the kitchen while I became the roaming observer of her domain.

Books were everywhere . . . on shelves, the floor, the kitchen counter, the chairs, the bed. It was obvious she was either reading fifty of them or simply liked the pleasure of their company, so she surrounded herself with them, like good friends. Mesmerized, I asked something profound like, "You enjoy reading, Edna?"

"Oh, yes, I love it. I'll never have enough time to read all I want, but I'm making a dent in my list. Some of these books I've had all my life. They're old and weathered . . . like me," she said laughingly, "but I can't ever throw them away. I can't even put them in a box. And I'm always adding new ones."

Edna did all her own cooking, housework, gardening, laundry, shopping — and seemingly loved every minute of it. That was the first of numerous times I went to see her. I finally didn't even drum up an excuse for showing up on

Sundays. I just liked Edna and the way she lived, and I wanted to be with her, learn from her, memorize how to be at any age.

She used to say little throwaways like, "While I'm making jam, I'm writing poetry in my head." Or "Planting flowers the other day, I worked on memorizing the first six Psalms." Or "I was standing at my kitchen window last week, when it hit me . . . *I think I'll paint the bathroom* . . . so I did." Or "I ran across a French word today while I was reading. Had to look it up so I could keep going."

What was Edna's secret? I've tried to figure it out, but have come to the conclusion that there wasn't one. She simply lived, and lived simply, every day . . . all the time. She integrated the whole of her life into everything she did, savoring her moments, counting her blessings, trying new things. Edna was Tasha Tudor, before her time.

If you want to have a life like that when you're eighty, you'd better start now. Here's what I recommend:

1. Stay spiritually centered with the Lord as your prime mover.
2. Learn something new every day and keep experimenting to make it better.
3. Wear your inside person outside, being who you really are.
4. Realize that tranquillity is your greatest source of beauty.
5. Remember God's mercies are new every morning . . . and *that* is grace.

> *However many years a man may live,*
> *let him enjoy them all.*
>
> ECCLESIASTES 11:8

❧

Sharing the Gift

Filled to Overflowing

BARBARA JOHNSON

❧

Some people grow up and spread cheer ...
others just grow up and spread.

Some of us are like cats; we don't know what we want, but we want more of it. Others are like dogs; we don't want much, and we are overjoyed when we get it. Regardless of our personality type or temperament, our Creator takes great delight in lavishing his extravagant grace upon us.

Sometimes grace comes as wisdom — or an empty parking space, a pat on the back, a beautiful sunset, an unexpected act of kindness. Grace might mean finding your lost dog, running into an old friend at the mall, or hearing a wacky joke that doubles you over with laughter. Grace is when the customer service department refunds your money, sends you another item without charge, even hands you a certificate for $10 off on your next purchase, then asks, "Is that satisfactory?" Grace turns the corners of your mouth up when things in life are trying to turn them down.

Grace is when whatever you need most comes at the moment you most need it. You need grace when your birthday cake collapses from the weight of the candles, and the bird singing outside your window turns out to be a buzzard. When you reach middle age and finally know your way around, you need grace because, by then, you won't feel like going! In my life, grace has appeared as humor and fun that make me feel lighthearted.

A friend of mine looked around her home one day and noticed something: every room contained several empty containers of different sizes and shapes. A tiny copper pitcher hung on a brass hook near the kitchen sink. A hand-glazed white pitcher was in the bathroom. An earthenware pot sat atop an antique cupboard in the living room. In her office, an odd-shaped jug served as a bookend. Pictures of empty jugs and pitchers even showed up in frames.

My friend realized these various containers were a metaphor for herself; she was an empty vessel waiting to be filled. She was thirsty for grace. Then she considered that each pitcher in her home was equipped with a pour spout. God seemed to be telling her that he wanted her to pour out his fullness into the lives of others. She wondered how effective she had been at doing that.

Surely, God's intention is that we overflow when he fills us to the brim! And it doesn't take a monumental feat to exercise grace toward others. It can be as simple as letting someone ahead of you in line. It can be saying to a sister in Christ, "Let me be your emotional bra." Grace always remembers that it's not your job to get people to like you, it's your job to like people.

You are only a decision away from pouring out grace. Here are some of its expressions:

"You did a good job."

"I was wrong."

"What do you think?"

"Thank you."

You can even say these to yourself, and cut yourself some slack. Everyone who got where she is had to begin where she was — including you!

Too many folks go through life running from something that isn't after them. They move too fast and yell too loud. But the poet Emily Dickinson wrote, "The soul should always stand ajar." Grace is all around and within you, just like my friend's empty vessels. So stand still awhile, your soul ajar. Notice grace. Appreciate it. As it flows into your open soul, drink deeply. And then from your fullness in Christ, pour out his grace on others.

From the fullness of his grace we have all received one blessing after another.

JOHN 1:16

🙿

Purple Grace

SHEILA WALSH

❧

What we practice, not (save at rare intervals) what we preach,
is usually our greatest contribution to the conversion of others.

C. S. LEWIS

As our plane touched down in Orlando, a delighted little smile tugged at the corners of my mouth. I knew my little boy was in for a treat—and I don't mean Mickey Mouse.

Barry and Christian and I were in Orlando to attend the annual House of Hope humanitarian awards dinner. I've been on House of Hope's advisory board for some time and have the deepest respect for the work that Sara Trollinger and her staff do in the lives of teenage runaway and "throwaway" boys and girls. Sara had asked me to sing at the banquet with the House of Hope girls backing me up. I was excited about the dinner, but also about the treat that Sara had arranged for Christian the morning of the banquet.

Sara's life philosophy is, "Come, let me show you how God loves you. Not tell you, but show you." From the first moment I met her as I conducted an interview with her and one of the girls from House of Hope on the *700 Club*, I knew that Sara was a very unusual woman. Most of us who live in cities across America know that some of our teenage kids are in trouble. We know the bad areas of town and we avoid them. But not Sara. With no money and a lot of faith, she founded the House of Hope, a refuge for hurting teens. Years later the statistics are staggering. More than 90 percent of those who graduate from her program have accepted Christ as Lord and leave with a fresh start in life.

At nine o'clock on the morning of the House of Hope banquet, Barry and I and our little lamb were waiting in the hotel lobby as Sara had instructed. I laughed when I saw a stretch limousine pull up for us out front. "How many people do you think ride in a limo to meet Barney?" I asked my equally amused husband.

For my little boy, meeting Barney of purple dinosaur fame was equivalent to me meeting someone like Billy Graham or Mother Teresa. When we arrived at Universal Studios, we were hooked up with Steve, our park guide for the day, and given front-row seats for the Barney stage show. When the lights went down and music started to play, Christian held my hand tight. Then, out of nowhere, with great fanfare and a huge cloud of smoke, appeared an eight-foot purple dinosaur! We knew all the songs (Oh, boy, do we know all the songs), and we sang along at the top of our voices. All too soon it was over. Or so we thought . . .

"Wait here," Steve said. The ushers cleared the building and then when no one else was left inside but us, out came Barney with his friends, B. J. and Baby Bop, to meet our little boy.

"Okay, forget Billy Graham," I whispered to Barry as Baby Bop was giving Christian a hug. "This is more like the Second Coming." Barry decided to let my irreverence go in the grace of the moment.

When it was finally time to carry our stunned child back to the car, I was nearly bursting with gratitude. "This is so like Sara to do this for us," I said to Barry. *So like God.*

As I stood on stage that night at the banquet and sang the words to my song, "God Is Faithful," I had a whole new appreciation for the many ways those words are true. Standing behind me were girls who just a year before were addicted to crack cocaine, living rough on the streets, in danger every night. Now they stood in lovely evening dresses and sang of the faithfulness of God. As the evening progressed, several teens stepped forward to share some of their stories. Woven through the heartbreak of their tales was a common thread: each girl and boy said they first encountered the love of God in the eyes of a woman named Sara Trollinger.

We all can't do what Sara does. But wherever God has placed us, let us pray that the grace of God is so rich in us that everything we say and do will shout the message, "Come, let me show you how God loves you."

He has showed you, O man, what is good.
And what does the LORD require
of you? To act justly and to love mercy and
to walk humbly with your God.

MICAH 6:8

❧

Gracious Lips

BARBARA JOHNSON

❧

I know you believe you understand what
you think I said, but I am not sure you realize that
what you heard is not what I meant.

God is great in great things," claimed Henry Dyer, "but very great in little things." Take lips, for instance. Because they're small, we don't think about them much; but I'll bet we all agree they are one of God's better ideas.

Webster's dictionary defines lips as organs of speech. The apostle Paul exhorted us, "Let your conversation be always full of grace" (Colossians 4:6). Perhaps Paul had read Rodale's *Synonym Finder* and been struck by these less than gracious synonyms for "lip": impudence, insolence, sauciness, sassiness, disrespect, derision, audacity, brazenness. Other often-used expressions about lips are fairly negative as well: bite the lips, button the lips, smack the lips, keep a stiff upper lip, give lip service.

But the lips are much more than just organs of speech that must overcome a lot of negative press in order to find grace. "To be on the lip of" is an expression connoting danger or opportunity; it means to be on the edge, the verge, or the brink of something. I like that. It brings to mind the idea of suspense, anticipation, and excitement.

On the human face, there is plenty of exciting work for lips to do. They are given nearly the same prominence as eyes because they are capable of expressing a wide range of emotions. Lips can display everything from anger to ecstasy. They can quiver in fear, tremble with tears, open wide in laughter, bid welcome with a bright smile, or express contempt with rigid tension. That set of little muscles is capable of wide extremes of action and influence. Lips can criticize a child, then kiss him off to school. They might nag a spouse, then hope for the passionate press of his lips. Be careful how you use those lips, but be thankful you have them!

Perhaps the best reason for lips (next to kissing, keeping insects from flying in, and spit from flying out) is that they were designed to smile. Smiling releases endorphins, those feel-good hormones that rush through the brain. Scientists say that even a forced smile makes you feel uplifted and less sad. Smiling even when you don't feel like it helps you handle stress. Here's why: The body associates pleasant sensations with that natural reflex of a smile. Your brain responds to the act of smiling, not the reason for it, and you actually feel better even if your circumstances haven't changed. Now if that isn't grace, I don't know what is!

The process of smiling or forming speech begins elsewhere in the body, of course: in your mind and heart, where ideas and emotions are born. Thoughts and feelings rush to the voice box and tongue, then pass through the changing shapes of the lips. When God touches our lips with grace, those little organs can heal sadness with kind words, or invite friendship with no words at all, just a smile. Someone has said, "Little things are the hinges on which great results turn." Gracious lips stimulate love, happiness, and health. Lips can keep complaints, criticism, and condemnation from passing into the world and harming someone's soul. So your lips are little hinges that God can use to achieve great results in his kingdom.

I once knew a woman who tried hard to please her irritable husband. One morning she went out of her way to prepare his favorite breakfast, arranging it on a tray with a linen napkin and rosebud. The coffee was hot, the toast crisp, the sausage well done just the way he liked it. The eggs were cooked to his specifications: one scrambled and one fried. As she set the tray before him, the man exclaimed, "Well, if you didn't scramble the wrong egg!"

Think twice before you use your lips for the wrong reasons! Use them to encourage, excite, enthuse, and inspire people. Use them to express true affection. A Swedish proverb exhorts: "Fear less, hope more; eat less, chew more; whine less, breathe more; talk less, say more; hate less, love more; and all good things are yours." Pray that each time you smile or speak, breathe or eat, pray or kiss someone, the power of your lips will be maximized by grace. Grace to you as you use those little organs of blessing!

> *You are the most excellent of men and*
> *your lips have been anointed with grace,*
> *since God has blessed you forever.*
>
> PSALM 45:2

～

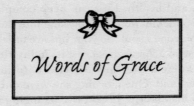

Words of Grace

SHEILA WALSH

*To the saint, personal insult becomes the occasion of revealing
the incredible sweetness of the Lord Jesus. . . .
The disciple realizes that it is his Lord's honour that
is at stake in his life, not his own honour.*

OSWALD CHAMBERS

The lovely fragrance of my great-grandmother's life blessed everyone who knew her. She had an enormous impact on my mother's life and, as a result, on mine. Mum tells me she can't remember one negative thing my great-grandmother ever said about anyone.

In fact, it used to make my mum mad. She'd come home from school hurt by some girl who had been mean to her and tell Gran all about it, expecting some sympathy and an opportunity to castigate the beast at school. But Gran would suggest that she pray for her instead. "You never know what's going on in her heart, Betty," she would say. "Perhaps things aren't too good at home."

Gran's consistently gracious attitude taught my mother to look beyond what seemed to be true and extend grace to graceless places. This rich legacy was passed on to me as a child. I now know that we had very little money as I was growing up, but I was almost never aware of it then because of the way my mum faced each day with joy and hope. That's what I want to pass on to my son.

Paul calls us to be above the negativity and small-mindedness of the world when he exhorts us, "Let your conversation be always full of grace, seasoned with salt, so that you may know how to answer everyone" (Colossians 4:6). What an impact it would have on our lives, our families, and the world if all our words were seasoned with grace!

Grace sees behind the scenes and takes in the whole picture. I recall a conversation I had with a woman in a Christian bookstore a few months ago. I had just released a book called *Life Is Tough But God Is Faithful.* I was in Houston, Texas, for a conference and had been asked by a local bookstore manager if I would drop by on the evening before the event to sign some books and meet a few customers. I was happy to, as it gave me a chance to find a new "Veggietales" video for Christian. I knew that if I heard "God Is Bigger Than the Boogie Man" one more time, I might lose it!

I was aware of the woman before she reached me in line. She looked angry and troubled. In the past I would have felt threatened by someone who looked as if they had a bone to pick with me. That was before I had received enough grace to understand that everything in life is not about me! That was before I learned to listen behind the words.

She loomed in front of me. "I heard the title of your new book on the radio," she said.

"Oh, really," I answered. "What did you think of it?"

"I wanted to slap you!" she replied.

"Why?" I asked, looking into her pain-filled eyes.

"Because my life is falling apart," she said. "My husband left me. I have two kids who need me. I'm struggling to make it through one more day, and you write some nice little Christian book called *Life Is Tough But God Is Faithful!*"

I felt such empathy for her. I could see that her soul was bleeding. I took her in my arms and held her as she wept out some of the bitterness and disappointment of her life.

"I am so sorry," I said. "I'm so sorry that your life has left you at this bus stop with no ticket to anywhere else."

She pulled back and looked at me for a moment. "I'm not really angry with you."

"I know that."

"I just hurt so bad, I don't know what to do."

Later we talked for nearly an hour. I didn't have answers for her questions or salve enough for her pain. All I could do was listen and weep with her.

That night, when I was in bed, I thought back to the days before my life fell apart, and I ended up in a psychiatric ward. I imagined my encounter then with a woman in that kind of pain, who only knew how to strike out. I realized that all I would have seen was someone attacking me. I would have missed the aching soul behind the words. Since those dark days in my own life, I have learned that when, at your lowest moment, you are gifted with grace and acceptance, you are given fresh grace for others, too.

The pattern Gran followed throughout her life is one I long to imitate. I want to hear behind the harsh words and offer the healing salve of Christ's love. I want to see beyond myself to those who are drowning but can't find the right words to ask for help. I want to soak my conversations in words of grace that bring life and hope and healing.

A gentle answer turns away wrath.

PROVERBS 15:1

⁊

Cataplexy

MARILYN MEBERG

❧

*There is nothing but God's grace. We walk upon it;
we breathe it; we live and die by it.*

ROBERT LOUIS STEVENSON

The subject of computers seems to illicit a deeply felt
but broad range of emotions. There are those who
love their computers with such devotion they don't leave
home without them. There are others who love their computers on some days and hate them on other days. Their
feelings range from deep affinity to potent animosity.

I find this breadth of emotion fascinating as well as
mystifying. To me it is so simple to have only one emotion
regarding computers ... that of loathing. I have fussed
about my troubled relationship with the personal computer
in a number of other writings. However, I recently discovered a word that accurately describes the physical and
emotional condition created in me by computer proximity
or my attempt to use a computer.

The word is *cataplexy*. It means "a sudden state of
immobility caused by extreme emotional stimulus." I love
that word! It makes me feel so understood. There is such
security in knowing that a label exists for my affliction.

And yet there is no pleasure in the condition. Therefore, I've had to determine a way to avoid cataplexy at all costs.

Obviously, since my computer is the only stimulus in my life that provokes cataplexy, I need to keep my computer out of sight and out of reach. That avoidance guarantees my good health. A simple solution, but here's the problem: pride. I'm not only embarrassed by my cataplexy, I'm embarrassed that an electronic box can reduce me to such a state.

Most of the other women contributing to this book have generally loving, warm, reciprocal relationships with their computers. When we come from all corners of the U.S.A. for planning meetings, each whips out an extension cord, claims her very own wall socket, and plugs in. In the midst of all this preparatory frenzy, I'm rifling through my purse in an effort to find a pen just in case I too might take notes during the meeting. This is hard on my pride, but I've managed to bear up under it. My techie friends are kind.

But just last week I experienced a breakthrough that will not only eliminate all future threat of cataplexy but of humiliation as well. (By the way, humiliation has its root in pride.)

My dear friend Patsy, who for six months of the year lives only one street away from me, wandered into my house on Wednesday. She stopped dead in her tracks (much like our dog Ashley used to do when we rearranged the furniture). Staring at the object on my counter she said, "What's that?"

"It's a typewriter. You may remember seeing one at the Smithsonian when we were in Washington, D.C., last winter."

"Ummmmm, do you use it for something, Marilyn?"

Reluctantly I confessed that when writing a book, I first scratch my thoughts out on a yellow legal pad. Then I type my scratches on my typewriter. I give my typed pages to my friend Pat, who retypes my words into her computer, and they end up on a square doo-dad. But she also sends them somehow to the computer of my editor, where they wait to be discovered.

Patsy's look of compassion as she listened to the pitiful rendering of my writing process nearly reduced me to tears. "Honey," she said, "you wait right here. I'll be back in three minutes. I want to read you something."

She returned with a magazine about how to write and publish fiction. From it she read to me the experience of a best-selling fiction writer who cannot bear computers and is terrified that typewriters will one day cease to be manufactured. This author literally stockpiles typewriters from Staples. (I had just purchased my third typewriter the day before Patsy dropped by.) The writer went on to say that she doesn't want to lose any of her crossed-out words from her legal pad in case she should decide later to use them after all.

Yahoo! My feelings exactly! I've rummaged through discarded scratchings a thousand times, convinced that whatever it was I wrote an hour ago is better than what I wrote two seconds ago. A computer would disdainfully destroy my scratchings forever. The yellow pad gently and without judgment preserves them for me in the event that I might someday want them. So nurturing.

When I finished that little therapy session with Patsy, my shame was banished and my dignity was restored! She extended to me a most wonderful and refreshing cup of grace. She didn't even hint that I was pitiful, technologically challenged, or hopelessly behind the times.

Instead, Patsy encouraged me by comparing my archaic writing methods with those of one who just happens to be a best-selling author and with whom I might one day fight over the world's last remaining typewriter!

Patsy, your style reminds me of God's.

> *God is our Light and our Protector.*
> *He gives us grace and glory.*
>
> PSALM 84:11 (TLB)

❧

Dressed to Kill

PATSY CLAIRMONT

❧

God's grace is the oil that fills the lamp of love.
HENRY WARD BEECHER

Today Les and I lunched at a charming French café. It was a delicious day, the kind you want to go on forever. The weather was perfect with enough warmth to sizzle and enough breeze to soothe. The food was scrumptious, and our table was situated outside under a wide striped awning. Music danced among the patrons, encircling us with cheery French sentiments. We drank in our surroundings of mountains in the distance, palm trees, and people nearby. Les and I chatted casually while we applauded the flaky French pastries and mused over the birds that dined on crumbs at our feet. We were delighted with the Paris ambiance, and we were pleased with each other.

Eventually, I decided to walk down the street to visit a couple of my favorite gift shops. (I have several in each city and in each state of the Union.) Les agreed to meet me in about thirty minutes at a certain store.

As I made my way to one of "my" shops, I realized the temperature was rising. The material of my beige outfit was a little weighty, and I was feeling the heat.

Then something caught my eye: a display of cool summer outfits surrounded by snappy accessories. The next thing I knew I had drifted inside and was trying them on. Wouldn't you know it? I looked darling. In fact, I was so cute I had the saleswoman clip all the tags off the outfit so I could wear it out the door. I then spotted a chipper yellow hat that would just top off the look, so I added it to the bill.

As I passed other store windows on my way to meet my husband, I caught sight of my new reflection and giggled, imagining Les's reaction.

I sashayed into the store and spotted Les chatting with the owner. Les glanced in my direction and started to turn away when something told him to look again. His head swiveled back and, as he took another gander, an incredulous look galloped across his face as he realized I was his beloved lunch date, the woman he thought he knew.

Oh, did I fail to mention that the outfit's screaming vibrancy made me look like an escapee from Ringling Brothers? Either that or I had bumped into a nauseated clown. Also, I don't wear hats.

I wish I could have recorded that moment. Les did decide to keep me, and I'm grateful.

Isn't that what happens so often in relationships? Just when we think we have someone figured out, she changes. Change is often startling, even scary. Yet many times, it's good. Change can be confusing, too. We think, *Why would anyone change when everything seemed to be going so well?* And change is usually jarring. I think change takes grace for all involved, because even the most positive kinds of change, uh, change things.

I remember when I first made a personal commitment to Christ, my decision changed me in many ways. While most of those changes pleased my husband, some of my new behavior and beliefs annoyed him. Suddenly I didn't appreciate Les's colorful humor, and he didn't appreciate my judgmental attitude. I didn't like his beer (and all it represented), and he didn't like my control issues. I stopped smoking and decided he should, too. He decided I should mind my own business.

I desperately needed God's grace for my deficient life, and I needed to experience grace to know how to extend it to others — like my beloved husband. When a person changes, it takes time for those around her to adjust and figure out what that means to their relationship. We complicate the adjustment to our change when we insist on trying to take everyone with us. Truth is, we can't change other people; only God can do that.

We can, though, extend grace to them. Grace is the space that allows others to grow or not grow, to agree or disagree, to change or remain unchanged. No wonder grace is a gift from God; left on our own, we humans just don't have that kind of spacious room inside us.

When we understand the great value in grace, then even when those around us show up dressed to kill, we won't. Instead, we will share the gift that God has so graciously bestowed upon us.

We have this treasure in jars of clay to show that this all-surpassing power is from God.

2 Corinthians 4:7

~

Grace at Home

THELMA WELLS

Learn to lavish the grace of God on others. Be stamped with God's nature, and His blessing will come through you all the time.

OSWALD CHAMBERS

had been taught from kindergarten on that you should pray for what you want, and God will give it to you. Well, at the time, I didn't know that wasn't the entire picture, but I did believe that God would listen to my heart's every wish. So in my early teens I started praying for God to send me a good husband.

When George Wells walked into my Sunday school class in January of 1956, I knew before I even met him that he was the one. I waited every Sunday to see this special young man. When I turned fifteen, my granny let George come over to visit, but she sat in the living room with us while we played Chinese checkers over and over again. No hanky-panky for Thelma!

Finally, six years later, George and I were married. We've been married for nearly forty years now, and life gets sweeter every year. My husband is a man among men. My relationship with him is one where love, understanding, happiness, peace, comfort, pleasure, and intimacy is lavished upon me — no strings attached.

But George is not a saint — and neither am I. Like every other couple, we've had some rough times and we've walked on some shaky ground. People sometimes ask me what our "secret" is to staying happily married for so long. Well, there is no question in my mind that the most crucial ingredient to a successful relationship is God's grace. Grace is the glue that keeps George and me together, and it is pure gift. But God also taught us long ago to be gracious to one another. By practicing the art of extending grace at home, we have avoided many of the heartaches we've watched other couples suffer.

It wasn't always like that. In the early years of our marriage, we argued a lot. (That's a nice way of saying we were at each other's throats on too many occasions to count!) Thangs weren't purty. After one particularly vicious fight, George approached me and asked me to promise him that we would not argue again. If either of us found ourselves getting "hot under the collar," we would agree to call a "time out" and separate until we cooled down.

With an "attitude," I agreed, thinking George would never follow through. But much to my surprise, he did just what he had suggested. The next time things started to get heated, he went out to his car and drove off until he thought I'd cooled off. I fumed up a storm while he was gone, but by the time he got back I was ready to act like an adult and talk things out rationally. Instead of continuing to inflict wound upon wound, as we'd always done, we began to respond rather than to react. Grace and peace began to reign in our home.

It's been over twenty years since George and I have had a fight. Now, I didn't say we've never been angry with each other in those twenty years; I said we haven't fought. You see, you can disagree but remain agreeable. Ruth Bell Graham's wise words apply in every marriage: "It's my job to love Billy. It's God's job to make him good."

One of my earliest "practice sessions" around this concept occurred when one of our daughters asked George if she could attend a slumber party. I'd already given her permission, never dreaming that George would say no. So we were both stunned when he said, "Absolutely not! I will not have a daughter of mine spending the night in somebody else's house. You don't know what's going on in somebody else's house."

Practicing being "agreeable" was not easy in that moment! Especially while I watched my baby cry, "Why, Daddy? Why? Why are you so mean, Daddy?" My heart was breaking for her, and I was mad enough to hit him. I could not understand his reasoning. But I read a bumper sticker once that said, "If my husband and I agreed on everything, one of us would not be necessary." I could have simply defied George's decision and let our daughter go to the slumber party or, probably even worse, scolded him in front of her. But this would hardly have created a gracious atmosphere in our home. I chose not to say anything to George until I'd cooled off a bit, comforted our daughter, and gotten my husband to myself.

As part of our pact never to have another destructive argument, George and I had agreed never to go to sleep angry with each other. As the evening wore on, I knew that pledge was about to be tested. So I prayed. As hacked off as I was, I tried to consider how I would want to be approached if I were in my husband's shoes.

Finally, right before bedtime, I sat down next to George and said, "Honey, you are a good father, and I know you would never hurt our children deliberately."

Rather than telling him off, I asked him, "Tell me again why you made that decision about the slumber party. I'm just having a problem understanding it because I don't see anything wrong with it."

George vented. He laid out all his reasoning to me in detail, and by the grace of God I didn't interrupt once. But I kept praying for strength to keep still while George expressed various opinions I disagreed with at the time. Finally, I told him how much I appreciated his concern for our daughter. I also asked him to make another agreement with me for the future: when one of our children had a request, both Mom and Dad would discuss it first before making any hard and fast decision. George agreed.

When we got into bed that night, we weren't all lovey-dovey, but at least we had successfully broken the habit of inflicting more damage on one another whenever we disagreed. As upset as I was with George at the time, I chose to extend grace to him the way I would have wanted him to extend it to me.

Since then, my husband and I have spent decades developing a new habit: treating each other the way God treats us. And you know what? It's really not as hard as we thought it would be!

> *Get rid of all bitterness, rage and anger, brawling and slander, along with every form of malice. Be kind and compassionate to one another, forgiving each other, just as in Christ God forgave you.*
>
> EPHESIANS 4:31–32

We're All Toads

BARBARA JOHNSON

☙

*Aren't you glad God loves us for what we are . . .
and not for what we should be?*

*D*o you remember the story of the princess with the
golden ball, and the toad who tormented her? In the
popularized version of the fairy tale by the Brothers
Grimm, the princess kisses the toad and voilà! The toad
turns into a prince.

Most of us identify with the toad in this story, hoping
to be kissed by a princess and be rescued from toad-ness.
But that was not the original ending. In the original version, the princess gets fed up with the toad's demands,
picks him up, and hurls him headlong against the palace
wall. Splat! Encountering the wall — encountering
truth — toad becomes prince.

An encounter with truth is what changes you and me
into royal beings who are full of grace. And one of the
most soul-transforming truths is looking in the mirror and
discovering that we're ordinary toads — with warts just
like everyone else.

I sometimes wear a little button that says, "Someone
Jesus loves has AIDS." By wearing it, I remind myself

that any kind of outcast deserves my compassion, not my judgment. Jesus said, "Don't condemn those who are down; that hardness can boomerang!" (Luke 6:37 THE MESSAGE). We all have problems and hang-ups. Grace is at its best when it's shared with the least loved or most undeserving.

Have you ever considered that the very last words in the Holy Bible are about grace? The beloved apostle John's last recorded statement is, "The grace of the Lord Jesus be with God's people. Amen" (Revelation 22:21). Paul knew all about the "toad-ness" inherent in God's people (he claimed he was the ugliest toad of all). And he knew that what we most need in order to represent Christ on earth is grace.

Jesus knew that, too, which is why he modeled it for us in everything he did. He mingled with all kinds of people, and he loved them all. I wonder, did those who loved him back always go on to live triumphant, glorious lives? Were they always courageous evangelizers? Did each of their offspring grow up to be successful and popular? Did they overcome all of their personal weaknesses? What about the double-minded Peter? The doubter, Thomas? The betrayer, Judas? Even Jesus was considered a criminal at the end of his young life. Does accepting Jesus as Lord mean that your life will be forever perfect?

In Jesus' day, many people believed sickness was a result of sin in a person's life. Religious people especially shied away from cripples or lepers, thinking they had brought misfortune on themselves. Whether or not that was true didn't matter to Jesus. He healed as many as called on him. He forgave them, too.

The truth is, we are all born naked, wet, and hungry. Then things get worse. We all need grace at its best!

Grace is simply knowing all about someone and loving them just the same. Jesus extends that grace to us every moment — and his Spirit in us enables us to graciously overlook the unbecoming, understand the unconventional, tolerate the unpleasant, overcome the unexpected, and outlast the unbearable in ourselves and other people.

Splat! That is grace in action. Grace is God's reality check in a phony-baloney world. When we no longer deny that we're ordinary toads, we don't need to judge anyone for living in a scummy pond instead of a palace garden, for we have been there, too. We offer grace to all the way King Ahasuerus extended the golden scepter to Queen Esther as a token of acceptance and mercy (Esther 8:4). We don't have to patronize anyone. We just accept toads, lepers, the homeless, AIDS victims, the mentally ill, and our next-door neighbor.

Remember, friend, your arms are the only ones God has to hug other people, and he may want to use your lips to kiss a few toads. Let him. And pray that each time you err in discernment, it may be on the side of grace!

May the grace of the Lord Jesus Christ,
and the love of God, and the fellowship of the
Holy Spirit be with you all.

2 CORINTHIANS 13:14

∾

Open Arms

SHEILA WALSH

෭

*Grace means primarily the free forgiving love of God in Christ
to sinners and the operation of that love in the lives of Christians.*

A. M. HUNTER

June 1981 was a dark time for many in America. A
new disease was officially recognized. It was called
GRID (Gay Related Immune Deficiency). The name
eventually was changed to AIDS (Acquired Immune
Deficiency Syndrome) when it was discovered that the
virus could be transmitted not only sexually but also by
blood transfusion or intravenous drug use.

I served for some time on the board of a ministry called
HIV (He Intends Victory). I studied all I could to understand this twentieth-century leprosy, but it was more than
an academic exercise for me. I had two friends who were
HIV positive. One of them was in the last stages of AIDS.
Each time his blood was monitored, his T-cell count was
down again. (This is one of the ways that doctors can
measure the rate at which the disease is stampeding
through a person's body.) My friend had only fifty T-cells
left. He named the final one "Judas."

The church has found it hard to deal with this disease. Is it God's punishment on godless behavior, as some would suggest? If that's true, then is breast cancer God's punishment for women? We seem so much more comfortable attributing blame than reaching out with the love and grace of God. I know that there are some inviolate principles in the universe, and it's true that we reap what we sow. That is the law. But Christ stepped into our human existence, and grace and redemption came with him. He fulfilled all the requirements of the Law on our behalf so that we could escape the fatal consequences of our sin.

When I served on that HIV board, three of the members, two men and a woman, were HIV positive. One of the men had contracted the virus through homosexual relations with an infected partner. The other man was a hemophiliac and got the virus in a blood transfusion before the nation's blood supply was as carefully monitored as it is now. The woman got it through an unprotected promiscuous lifestyle.

It became clear to me as I served beside these brothers and sisters in Christ that how they got the disease was irrelevant. God's grace is sufficient for all situations. If we don't believe that, then we render Calvary limited in its power to redeem. Every man, woman, and child who walks this earth is indelibly imprinted with the image of God. We can hold up the standard of a righteous way of life, but we have to leave room for those who are suffering to lay their head on our breast. As God's children we have a divine mandate to extend grace to those in need. Christ himself was our model as he fulfilled his Father's mission on earth: "He has sent me to bind up the brokenhearted, to proclaim freedom for the captives and release from darkness for the prisoners, to proclaim the year of the LORD's favor and the day of

vengeance of our God, to comfort all who mourn, and
provide for those who grieve in Zion — to bestow on
them a crown of beauty instead of ashes, the oil of glad-
ness instead of mourning, and a garment of praise
instead of a spirit of despair" (Isaiah 61:1–3).

The "live any way you like" mentality has seriously
backfired on a generation of baby boomers. So how will
we as the church respond? This is a time for grace. Surely
this is a time to share the gift. If we would stand with open
arms and welcome the broken and the bruised into the
family, we would then begin to understand redemption.

Dear friends, since God so loved us,
we also ought to love one another.
No one has ever seen God; but if we
love one another, God lives in us and
his love is made complete in us.

1 JOHN 4:11–12

✒

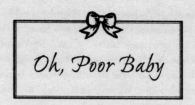

Oh, Poor Baby

PATSY CLAIRMONT

❧

The grace you had yesterday won't do for today.

OSWALD CHAMBERS

My mom, Rebecca, grew up on a Kentucky farm. She was the youngest of six children and was nicknamed "Sister." (I guess their nicknaming creativity ran thin by number six, or perhaps because my mom was such a petite munchkin, "Sister" just seemed to fit her.)

Mom told me that her family never had a lot of material possessions, but they were well fed because they ate from the farm's bounty. When the Great Depression hit, they didn't feel the impact to the degree that many others did because they worked for themselves and could rely on their crops. But they knew all about putting in a hard day's work in the fields. They also suffered painful loss when my grandmother died, leaving behind a young, grieving family.

During my grandmother's lingering illness, a woman of prayer stopped by for a visit. My mother was seated nearby when the woman noticed that Sister's little-girl hands were covered in hundreds of warts. The woman called my mother to her side and embraced her hands. At one point the woman stroked Mom's hands and said, "Oh, poor baby . . . oh, poor baby." Clasping them once more in her own hands, the woman said her good-byes and left.

Over the next several days the warts began to fall off my mother's hands until, within a week, all the warts were gone, never to return.

Many times my mom has retold this story to me. She said the woman didn't say she was praying while she touched Mom's hands, but my mother sensed it even at her young age. Mom believes that the Lord answered this woman's prayers and healed a little girl's hands.

I'm impressed that the woman touched my mother's hands and embraced them with such tenderness. Often, I find, when people aren't as we think they should be, we tend to withdraw — which is a hoot when we realize almost nothing in this life is without flaw. But our human nature is to pull back physically, emotionally, and relationally when we encounter defects in another. We don't always know how to respond to what seems abnormal to us — unless, like the woman of prayer, we have experienced God's grace for the abnormalities in our own lives. For I believe God's grace enables us not to be alarmed, frightened, or repelled at humankind's defectiveness.

This story also reminds me that ministry to others doesn't have to be announced or showy. The woman never said, "Kneel, child, I'm about to pray." Yet my mother sensed the woman's spirit of faith as well as her merciful approach. I believe this woman had experienced God's grace in her life, for we can't give away to others something we don't have.

The story of Anna, whose very name means "grace," is found in the New Testament. She experienced God's grace when she became a widow after only seven years of marriage. We know that loss has the potential to cause us to shrivel or shine depending on how we embrace our sadness and his provision. Anna became a noted woman of prayer, praise, and prophecy and remained faithful more than eighty years in this ministry until she beheld the Christ child. Anna shone.

A grace-filled woman is one who extends herself to others with sensitivity, mercy, good taste, and insight. Anna and the woman of prayer in my mother's life spent much time in God's grace-filled presence. That's why a "sister" could sense the spirit of prayer operative in one life and how, in the other, Anna could live alone for eighty years and still shine brightly for the Lord.

Maybe this explains why my light is flickery, why my well of mercy is more like a puddle than a pool, why good taste and sensitivity are sometimes erased by my reactive personality, and why my insights vary in value. I, for one, need to get down on my knees and not get up until I embrace more of his extravagant grace.

Let us then approach the throne of grace with confidence, so that we may receive mercy and find grace to help us in our time of need.

HEBREWS 4:16

❧

Smoke Travels

MARILYN MEBERG

God's grace makes us worthwhile and valuable for who we are, and not because of what we successfully accomplish.

DAVID SEAMANDS

*O*ne of my childhood heroes was a woman I met only once. She wore outlandishly bright colors and spiked high-heeled shoes, sported mounds of dyed red hair, and, most memorable, belched frequently. She was married to the conference superintendent, one of the local administrators of the church denomination in which my father pastored.

I met Mrs. Justin when she and Dr. Justin came to our home for dinner. My mother had coached me ahead of time, warning that Mrs. Justin had some kind of digestive difficulty that caused her to belch whenever the need should arise. When that happened, I was not to wheel around and stare, or giggle. That was a tall order, but I promised.

Dr. Justin had already presented a challenge to my self-control on two occasions when he had guest-pastored at Dad's church. He wore the worst-looking toupee one could imagine. Not only was gleaming scalp visible under its ill-fitting edges, but it was never centered — a fact that mystified me. To my child logic, it seemed perfectly simple for him to center the hairpiece by using his nose as a marker. Apparently that obvious solution had never been considered because the toupee consistently veered either to the left or the right, especially when he energetically expressed his sermon's main points.

When the Justins arrived for dinner, I was laboring under so many restrictions on my behavior that I felt tense. Mrs. Justin lived up to her belching reputation throughout the meal, but I was relieved to find that I didn't have any desire to giggle. There was something rather poignant about her. She never entered into any of the conversation but seemed instead to be in her own noisy little world. I ultimately decided she didn't have a digestive difficulty at all ... she was simply bored. I certainly was. But, of course, I didn't dare use her remedy.

At the conclusion of the meal I was excused to go upstairs to my room. My intention was to stretch out on my bed for a good read. As I switched on the radio, I saw the Lucky Strike cigarette I had scooped up from our neighbor's driveway the day before. Since the cigarette was so clean and tidy, I'd tucked it behind my radio ... perhaps for a time such as this. After all, I was still feeling a trifle tense, and people claimed to feel more relaxed after a cigarette. Maybe I needed that more than my book.

I'd never smoked, and it didn't occur to me that any particular skill was necessary. As I lit the cigarette and drew the smoke into my mouth, I didn't know what to do next. Involuntarily I gagged and coughed as smoke came out of every orifice above my neckline. *How do people get the smoke to exit only through their nostrils in that steady trail that looks so effortless?* I wondered. Try as I might, I could only spew ghastly billows of smoke from my mouth. I was not finding this a pleasant activity, and it certainly wasn't relaxing me. In fact, I was feeling increasingly nauseous and lightheaded.

It never crossed my mind that the smoke would slip under my closed door, glide down the stairs, and quietly enter the living room where Dr. Justin sat talking church business with my parents. It wasn't until my mother's disapproving face appeared at my door that I realized I might soon be facing an indictment.

Shortly after, I was invited downstairs to say good-bye to the Justins. As I awkwardly shook hands with each of them, Mrs. Justin leaned down and whispered in my ear, "Don't worry about your smoking, Honey. I started at an early age myself."

I realize now that Mrs. Justin was probably as off-center as her husband's toupee, but nonetheless she extended unexpected grace to me. In that era, smoking was considered completely taboo by most Christians. What Mrs. Justin's comment did for me was to make me feel still connected to others instead of ostracized as a smoking little sinner.

My brief exchange with the belching but gracious Mrs. Justin provided an early lesson about God's grace and God's family. I believe that one of the best ways we extend the gift of grace is by remaining connected to others when they blow it. God himself continues to love us with the same gracious intensity even when we fail. No matter how huge or small our transgression, he will absolutely stay with us, love us, encourage us, and lead us back to healthy behavior. That's what he wants us to do for each other.

Incidentally, I haven't smoked since.

*A bruised reed he will not break, and a
smoldering wick he will not snuff out.*

ISAIAH 42:3

❧

Shine, Shine, Shine!

PATSY CLAIRMONT

Hide it under a bushel? No! I'm gonna let it shine.

TRADITIONAL BLACK SONG

The older Les and I become the more we appreciate a well-lit path. We want to see where we're going as we bop from one room to another. (In the past, we've tripped over everything from vacuum cleaners to each other.) We also want light to see what we're reading without straining our bifocals or our brains. And we want to see to measure ingredients during our sporadic kitchen escapades — and I do mean sporadic.

The exception to this illuminating need in our lives would be the lighting around our morning mirror, the bedtime mirror, and, oh, yes, the daytime mirror. Some things are better left in the shadows.

Recently Les purchased some solar lights to place along our walkways and our patio. I was fascinated. These clever illuminators gather light during the day, store it, then shine like crazy at night. This eliminates the need for unsightly wires and electricity. These lamps are spiffy.

One night, high winds blew a couple of these lights off their pedestals and ping-ponged them around our patio. So Les brought them in and laid them on our dresser. Later, when I entered the dark bedroom, the pool of light emanating from the room's corner startled me. Even during off hours they continued to shine, shine, shine. Reminded me of the song "This Little Light of Mine."

Being touched by God's extravagant grace ignites something within us that causes others to notice. It's an interior glow that is like an exterior light in that it casts its influence in spite of the degree of darkness in which it finds itself — not only in spite of the darkness but also because of it. In the darkness the light becomes more attractive, more influential, more valuable, and more obvious.

Deborah, a judge in the Old Testament, was called to be a solar light during a time when spiritual darkness covered the land. She rose to the call, took a stand for truth, and stayed faithful even in the face of an intimidating enemy. God used this woman's life to redirect an entire nation's steps. Previously, the people were stumbling around in the darkness of their own poor choices, straining to walk in their own piteous ways, and measuring their behavior by their neighbors' behavior. They definitely needed a well-lit path; they needed some solar lights. Then Deborah, who gathered brilliance in God's presence, became his light-holder and his light-bearer — and she did it with strength and grace.

I've seen this type of dedication in my friend Thelma. She is a light-bearer of the brightest kind. Thelma has a bottomless reservoir of God's love for people that she lavishly sprinkles around. I enjoy watching Thelma's beaming face as she embraces the ladies in her hug lines at conferences. She enfolds folks in acceptance and guides them to our radiant Savior and his illuminating counsel.

I've watched Thelma send forth his light and shine, shine, shine.

I've also observed when Thelma has faced difficult days, times when the Prince of Darkness has tried to trip her up, and she has reached even deeper into her arsenal of God's light-giving truth. Thelma is a solar light who faithfully stores light while it is day. I have benefited from seeing the commitment in her life, for while Thelma is capable of feisty, what you see is faithful because of God's grace aglow in her soul. You shine, girlfriend!

What does it take to be a solar-powered sister? A relationship with Christ, a dedication to his Word, and God's brilliant grace. If you need greater clarification in your life, if you're uncertain what next step you should take, if you long to make a difference in your world, then invite Christ to bring the light of his life into your darkened understanding. If you've done that and still feel as if you're stumbling around, then redouble your efforts to be in his light-bearing Word. Gather up his truth, store it in your heart, and then shine like crazy.

Each one should use whatever gift he has
received to serve others, faithfully administering
God's grace in its various forms.

1 Peter 4:10

Celebrating
the Gift

Guatemala Gals

LUCI SWINDOLL

❧

*The experience of God's grace cannot be manufactured, you see.
There is no technique available that will lead you to it.*

PAUL TOURNIER

I have to say I am *impressed* with World Vision. It's an international Christian relief agency that helps the poor all over the world by meeting needs in emergencies, development, training, and education. Because World Vision is in partnership with Women of Faith, we have an opportunity to see firsthand the work they're doing and to be actively engaged in their outreach.

One such occasion occurred in January 1999 when several of us flew to Guatemala to participate in their child sponsorship program. I have to admit, I was a little nervous before going. I was asked to sign a form disavowing World Vision from almost anything that could happen to me — injury, damage to my person or property, acts of terrorism, violence, kidnapping, hostage-taking. Little things like that! But I'm an adventurer at heart so I thought, *why not?* I signed, packed my bag, and headed for Central America.

Guatemala is a beautiful country. From my hotel window I could see two volcanoes (one was active with smoke billowing out). *Please!* There are bustling cities, colorful villages, jungles, highlands, lakes, and people with flawless brown skin and ready smiles. But there's a lot of sorrow behind all this beauty. Because the poverty level is high and incomes low, young Guatemalan girls have little chance of getting even the most basic education. It is in addressing this problem that World Vision finds one of its greatest challenges and highest achievements.

In spite of obvious deprivation, however, everywhere we went we saw happy individuals living lives of apparent fulfillment. One family had lost the roof of its house in Hurricane Mitch, yet they were so pleased we were there, nothing else mattered. The entire neighborhood turned out to watch us make tortillas. Patty cake, patty cake . . . it looked so simple but, as we discovered, it is a real art form. My tortillas were shaped just like Guatemala. Oh, well.

In one little hamlet, several miles from the capital city, World Vision has a very enterprising program where they make bank loans to Christian women, helping them improve their quality of life. Some of these women set up retail operations in their homes, others raise poultry or sell crafts.

When I met one of the women (a mother of two children) who had been given a loan to maintain a small chicken farm, I asked her which was harder — raising children or chickens. To my surprise, she said, "They're the same . . . each demands tenderness and responsibility. If you aren't careful to meet their needs, the baby chicks will die. It's the same with children."

What a great answer! I thought she'd say, "Oh, children, of course," but she didn't. She understood commitment — and the hard relentless work of tending to the needs of those in your care. I loved her reply. No nonsense. No phony philosophical platitudes. Real life.

Since then, I've had time to reflect on our visit to Guatemala, and I've realized that there was a time when I might have seen people with little of this world's goods, eking out an existence or struggling to make ends meet, and thought, "There but for the grace of God go I." In fact, I've said that many times. But no more. What that statement reveals is an attitude of, *I'm the recipient of more grace than they are. Look at what I have! God's been better to me than he has been to them.* That is simply not true. In fact, it's a very distorted view of grace.

Sometimes we have the mistaken idea that God loves and blesses us more if we look, live, or behave a certain way. If our lives are tidier, he's happier. If we are "successful" in the world's eyes, he's relieved. If we become cultured or erudite, he feels better about us. We assume God prefers designer clothes and custom homes. We presume he's pleased with fancy careers and technological advances. But in God's economy, grace doesn't work like that. God places *no* emphasis on externals. He looks at our hearts, and he blesses us from the inside out. His goodness is available to *all*.

Those Guatemala gals are wonderful reminders that God's grace is limitless. It's not dependent on anything we've done — or have. God gives us himself, in the person of Jesus Christ, and he does it whether we live in a New York City penthouse or under a thatched roof at the foot of a volcano. He loves us infinitely, with extravagant grace!

Praise the LORD. Give thanks to the LORD,
for he is good; his love endures forever.
Who can proclaim the mighty acts of the LORD
or fully declare his praise?

PSALM 106:1–2

Rejoice!

SHEILA WALSH

ॐ

The word grace emphasizes at one and the same time
the helpless poverty of man and the limitless kindness of God.
WILLIAM BARCLAY

"I think it would be a good idea if you could lose a few
pounds before the tour begins," my manager suggested gingerly.

Yeah, and I think it would be a good idea if you grew your hair
back! I thought to myself.

Bill Latham meant well. I was going on the tour of a
lifetime supporting British megastar Cliff Richard. Cliff
has never been well known in America, but in the rest of
the world he has sold more singles than The Beatles, The
Rolling Stones, and The Who all put together. (And no,
those are not Southern gospel quartets!) As well as being
a successful pop star, Cliff is also a very committed Christian. Once a year he would do a tour for a British relief
charity called Tear Fund, and this time I was the opening act.

I was humiliated by Bill's "suggestion," but I'll admit
I needed to lose weight. I don't mean I was huge. You
couldn't have shown *Ben Hur* on my posterior, but I defi-

nitely fell into the "chunky" category. I had tried for ages to lose the twenty pounds that I tucked into my jeans and under my sweater; but they were clingy little pounds and reluctant to be evicted from their cozy, well-fed home.

"I've tried to diet," I whined pathetically. "My pastor told me that if I would just carry all of my diet books up and down the stairs a few times I'd never have a weight problem again."

"I have a plan," Bill said with a look of confidence.

My heart sank.

"I'm enrolling you in a clinic in London for two weeks. They will exercise you and put you on a strict diet and work wonders." He beamed. "You'll be a new woman!"

Good grief! I thought.

"All you have to do is stick with the program. Will you do that?"

"Oh, yes," I said with all the fervor of an alcoholic with a fifth of Scotch hidden in her sweater.

When I arrived at the "clinic" (i.e., fat farm), I was weighed in by a skinny thing who looked like her clothes had been sprayed on to emphasize her tiny frame. I had to keep my mouth firmly clamped so I wouldn't blurt out what was on the tip of my tongue: "Listen, Bones, if it wasn't for people like me, you'd be out of a job!"

For the next two weeks, Bones and her friends wrapped me and pummeled me and starved me till I looked like a leftover turkey at the homeless shelter on Thanksgiving. Then came D-Day. I think of it as "Black Tuesday." I stood on the scale and could have shot the little traitor. I had gained four pounds!

That's just one of the humiliating moments in my history. I hated myself. I was so ashamed that I had no willpower. I felt ugly and unlovable. I imagined when people looked at me they saw a fat, unattractive girl because that's what I saw in the bathroom mirror . . . if I turned on the light.

But Christ didn't die so I'd continue to feel rotten about myself! Ephesians 2:13 tells me, "But now in Christ Jesus you who once were far away have been brought near through the blood of Christ." I spent many years as a believer, knowing I was pardoned for my sin but keeping a distance even from God because I didn't find myself worth loving. Every magazine I read showed images so far removed from my reality that I despaired of ever feeling worthy — until I was invited to a party with Cliff Richard and realized that all the so-called "beautiful people" were empty if they had no relationship with Christ. I sat and listened as Cliff shared his faith with people whose faces were well known to me. I watched as tears streamed down perfect makeup onto designer dresses. I realized how I had bought into the lies and despair of the world. I asked God to forgive me. I didn't need to be a "new woman" according to the world's ideas. I was already loved completely by God, as the woman I was.

When you look in a mirror, what do you see? Do you zero in on a crooked nose, a blemish, a sagging jaw, tired eyes packing their own bags? Have whole parts of your body moved to a new neighborhood? I encourage you as a fellow traveler to cherish and celebrate the gift of grace that calls you to draw near, to let go of your obsession with the shell of your life, and to fall more in love with Jesus. As women who have been drawn close to the heart of God by the embrace of Christ, you and I have the best reason of all to rejoice. Because God is near — no matter what.

> *Rejoice in the Lord always. I will say it again:*
> *Rejoice! . . . The Lord is near.*
>
> PHILIPPIANS 4:4–5

✷

Grace-full in His Sight

BARBARA JOHNSON

Hey, do you realize you are a miracle?
Someone like you will never happen again!

*H*ave you ever meditated on Scripture by putting your name in place of the personal pronouns or characters' names? I love to go through my Bible that way. The Word of God just seems to come alive.

Take, for example, Genesis 6:8 (KJV): "But Noah found grace in the eyes of the LORD." Put your name in place of Noah's. How might embracing that grace change the way you pray? How might it change your day?

Find as many verses as you can about grace and insert your name into the flow of the Scripture. Here are a few to get you started:

My grace is sufficient for _____ (2 Corinthians 12:9).

Grace is poured upon _____'s lips (Psalm 45:2 NKJV).

And great grace was upon _____ (Acts 4:33 KJV).

It is a great treat in my day when I imagine that God is seeing me covered, smothered, and smoothed over with extravagant grace. All my rough edges are rounded in grace. All my imperfections are hidden by grace. All my frayed ends are tied up with grace. All that I'm lacking is filled up with grace. How can I allow myself to fret and to worry, or to inflict guilt on myself, when I realize that in God's eyes I find grace upon grace (John 1:16)?

Don't you think we should delight in seeing ourselves the way God does? Then we can go out and share our best with the world. Our future is glorious in him because he has already said, "Have a good day and a fabulous forever!" He is growing us into saints. Though it may take a lifetime, shouldn't we rejoice along the way? Shouldn't we be grateful for how God is using us, even when the people around us might not appreciate it at the time?

My friend, remember to take this life one day at a time. When several days attack you, don't give up. A successful woman takes the bricks the Devil throws at her and uses them to lay a firm foundation. We all need enough trials to challenge us, enough challenges to strengthen us, and enough strength to do our part in making this a better place to live and love. Grace is receiving the gift of God in exactly who we are and bearing its fruit in the world. Just think how it changed the world because Noah didn't say, "I don't do arks." Moses didn't say, "I don't do seas." Paul didn't say, "I don't do letters." Michelangelo didn't say, "I don't do ceilings." Martin Luther didn't say, "I don't do doors." And, of course, Jesus didn't say, "I don't do crosses."

Some people can't afford the tuition for the school of hard knocks. But that's where grace comes in. When God believes in you, your situation is never hopeless. When he walks with you, you are never alone. When God is on your side, you can never *ever* lose. So don't be afraid of tomorrow; God is already there!

A darling woman wrote a letter to me about how finally, after many years of worrying about the unacceptable lifestyles of a son and daughter, she had learned to lay her son and daughter in God's hands. She wrote:

It seemed that forever all I did was beseech God's throne for these two. I read everything I could find on "letting go and letting God." At one of my lowest times, I told God that I needed to be ministered to . . . and for that one day I knew I could trust Him to take over these children that we both loved. Then I decided to set aside Friday each week for God to minister to my needs. I turn over anything I'm concerned about for at least that one day. I dress as attractively as I can, put on my favorite perfume, and do everything that comes to my mind that I feel God leading me to do. I praise and thank him all day long. It was the beginning of the return of joy into my life.

Isn't this a beautiful idea? Remember, you are bathed in grace. Get dressed and put on your favorite perfume. God expresses his grace in the miracle of *you* every single day. You are grace-full in his sight. Believe it. Now go out and dance for joy!

> *"Hear the word of the LORD, O nations;*
> *proclaim it in distant coastlands:*
> *'He who scattered Israel will gather*
> *them and will watch over his flock like*
> *a shepherd.' . . . Then maidens will dance*
> *and be glad, young men and old as well.*
> *I will turn their mourning into gladness;*

I will give them comfort and joy instead of sorrow.
I will satisfy the priests with abundance,
and my people will be filled with my bounty,"
declares the LORD.

JEREMIAH 31:10, 13–14

❧

Gone Fishing

LUCI SWINDOLL

❧

In my opinion, legalism is the greatest heresy of Christianity.
BILL BRIGHT

The sign "GONE FISHING" was a common sight on the door of my granddaddy's office. He had a successful insurance business in a small Texas town. But on certain occasions, nothing was more satisfying or more important to him than closing shop and heading toward the Gulf, rod and reel in hand. When he got word that the tide was in and the fish were biting, hardly anything could keep Granddaddy from the fine art of angling. In this field, he was a pro.

Not only was my grandfather into the sport of fishing, but my dad, a couple of uncles, some cousins, a brother, and even I loved to "reel 'em in and fry 'em whole." As a child I enjoyed these family outings, which at times occurred on a weekend, causing me to miss Sunday school and church. I rarely missed Sunday services, but a fishing trip with kith and kin was an excuse sanctioned by my parents. After all, I wasn't just playing hooky. I was doing something important.

My Sunday school teacher, Mrs. Borden (as in Lizzie) was a rather tight-jawed, strict, corseted woman in her sixties whose goal in life was to have perfect attendance week after week among her fledgling students. No excuse for being absent was acceptable. I rather hated her. Every Sunday I spent class time dreaming up ways to blow up her car. With her in it.

One unforgettable morning after I'd been absent the week before because of a family fishing trip, Mrs. Borden quizzed me in front of the entire class. "Where were you last Sunday, Lovell Lucille?" (I know . . . it's a family name).

Frightened of public ridicule but not wanting to lie, I whispered, "I went fishing with my family."

"You what? Speak up so we can all hear you."

"I went fishing. We all went . . . my granddaddy, mother, daddy, and two brothers."

"Well, now." Mrs. Borden smiled malevolently. "Do you think God can bless you when you aren't in his house on Sunday?"

I didn't know how to respond, so I just sat there, feeling sheepish and terribly embarrassed. Later I wished I'd said, "Of course She can, Axe-face." But I didn't think of it at the time.

Without apology, Mrs. Borden's eyes moved past me and on to the next student who had been absent the previous Sunday. He was openly questioned and criticized just as I had been.

I don't know what ever happened to Mrs. Borden (although I have a suspicion as to her present whereabouts), but I'll never forget that blatant display of legalism in her classroom. I've thought back on it many times, always with anguish for the indelible black smudge it left on my young soul.

You see, what legalism does is cling to the unbending letter of some artificial law at the expense of liberty in God's grace. It binds the Christian to performance and conformity. It kills the spirit. It robs one of the freedom there is in a relationship with Christ, thus forcing a particular behavioral code to be one's standard for living. What a shame!

Jesus Christ never taught that one person should tell another what to do, where to go, how to live. In fact, he reserved his harshest comments for those who tried. ("White-washed tombs" was his term for these know-it-alls!) Jesus said, "Follow me." He never instructed us to follow each other's rules. He never gave anyone control over another. His desire is that his Word and his Spirit be our guides for life. Being a follower of Jesus Christ means becoming more and more like him ... letting his Spirit transform us into all we were created to be. That happens, dear friend, from the inside out.

Unfortunately, there will always be Mrs. Bordens in the world, ready to pounce on anything that smacks of grace and freedom. They'll be standing in the wings of your life, waiting to make their entrance with demands, curfews, criticism, and rules. They're always close at hand, wanting to squelch the passion and pleasure of knowing the Savior. Don't let them. And, with all the love in the world, let me say: Don't be one! As a follower of Christ you have the unique opportunity every day to demonstrate and celebrate his grace.

I love Jesus Christ today in large part because of the gracious godly influence of my granddaddy who took me fishing — sometimes on Sundays.

> *It is for freedom that Christ has set us free.*
> *Stand firm, then, and do not let yourselves*
> *be burdened again by a yoke of slavery.*
>
> GALATIANS 5:1

ᴥ

Contagious Grace

Marilyn Meberg

❧

Grace is too unpredictable, too lavish,
too delicious for us to stay sober about it.

Lewis B. Smedes

On a recent Sunday morning, I was reminded of how contagious grace is when one believer lives it out in front of others. Sweet nostalgia swept over me as I joined the church congregation in singing "How Great Thou Art" under the direction of Cliff Barrows. My mind was flooded with memories of that dear man when, at least forty years before, I sang in the volunteer choir for the Billy Graham Crusade in Portland, Oregon, and then ten years later in the choir in Anaheim, California.

Now, with the same sweet spirit of one whose ministry and life so winningly radiates the grace of God, Cliff Barrows led us in some of the great hymns of faith. As we completed the last verse of "I Love to Tell the Story," Dr. Barrows stepped behind the pulpit, opened his Bible, and began his sermon. I was so aware that this man was an icon of the Christian faith, and I felt privileged to hear him. Coupled with these very genuine feelings of appreciation,

my memory served up an experience with Dr. Barrows
that I had not thought of in years.

I was chairman of Fullerton's Christian Women's Club
and thrilled that Dr. Barrows was to be our December
guest speaker. The night before that Christmas luncheon,
I was increasingly agitated as I tried to think of a worthy
introduction for this dearly loved man. Everything I
thought to say sounded so flat, so dull, so uninspiring. My
husband, Ken, tried to encourage me out of my dithering
state with phrases like "It'll come to you" or "It's only an
introduction, Marilyn."

When nothing came, I finally went to bed and drifted
into a most graphic and specific dream about the luncheon. In that dream, shortly after Dr. Barrows started
speaking, he slipped a little silver flask out of his breast
pocket. He took a quick sip and then replaced the flask.
Several times throughout his speech he repeated this little maneuver, and as his words became increasingly inco-
herent, everyone in the room began glowering at me as if
I were the one responsible for the flask and its effects.
One by one the women began gathering up their belong-
ings and, with withering expressions shot in my direction,
exited the room. Within a few moments Dr. Barrows and
I were the only two left. When he took full notice of that
fact, he patted my shoulder and said, "It's just as well,
Marilyn, my flask is empty anyway."

I awakened the next morning giggling over the
implausibility of Cliff Barrows' behavior depicted in my
dream. I asked Ken if he thought I could use it in my
introduction. With one of those "Are you out of your
mind?" looks, Ken swept on out of the house and headed
for work.

Several hours later as I stood to introduce Dr. Barrows, I decided to risk telling the dream. The women

enjoyed its obvious absurdity but were slightly restrained in their responses since they weren't sure how it was being received by Dr. Barrows. When he stood up, he first smiled warmly at everyone and then reached into his vest pocket, pulled out an imaginary flask, threw his head back, made a slurping sound, and sighed with satisfaction as his audience burst into peals of appreciative laughter. Everyone loved him! We loved not only his winsomely delivered, God-centered message but also his freedom to be playful and not hung up with images or appearances.

In direct contrast to his contagious freedom was the note slipped to me from a woman at the luncheon. She wrote that she felt joking about the flask was inappropriate for a Christian environment and that she was deeply offended. This was not the first note I had received from her, and certainly not the first criticism. It's quite possible that her grim-faced approach to life was rooted in some deep pain to which I'm not privy, but I find it sad that her life seems to revolve around the externals of what she perceives to be "the faith." Monitoring and reporting infractions of the "rules" keeps her more engaged than does the sweetness of God's grace.

I worry sometimes that we as believers are more concerned with the appearance of righteousness than with the inner acquisition of righteousness. Celebrating the gift of grace means freeing oneself from the shackles of performance and luxuriating in the circumference of God's lavish acceptance. Now that's a gift worth toasting!

I am come that they might have life, and that they might have it more abundantly.

JOHN 10:10 (KJV)

❧

Peanut Butter 'n Grace

BARBARA JOHNSON

The good life starts the moment you stop wanting a better one.

In our ministry, which I call Spatulaland (notice the La-La Land in that word?), we've met a great variety of personality types. Many expose their quirks without meaning to. One lady wrote, "The lab called with good news; they said my brain is ready!" A gentleman insisted, "My wife thinks I'm too nosy. At least, that's what she keeps scribbling in her diary." One woman told me she had been introduced to her husband at a travel agency. "I was looking for a nice vacation destination," she said, "and he was the last resort!"

I agree with what Christian author Mike Yaconelli says, "If we believed the truth we would allow it to explode in pockets of oddness all over this country. Somebody put it this way, 'You shall know the truth and the truth shall make you odd.'"

My husband, Bill, is a good example of odd. When he makes a peanut butter sandwich, he has to have the bumps match! As he spreads the nutty goo on his bread, he painstakingly moves and smoothes it until he achieves a uniform design. I guess it makes him feel secure. He seems not to mind that a swipe of peanut butter tends to end up on a finger or a thumb.

When God makes people different from each other, full of peculiarities, he proclaims his extravagant grace. Grace is God's exception to his own rules. When you think about it, the whole story of redemption breaks the rules. When Jesus Christ died on the cross, didn't God create an exclusion to the law of sin and death? When we receive Christ by faith, doesn't God forgive us even though we don't deserve it? Our salvation breaks all the rules of the universe. In our unique ways, you and I are extraordinary examples of God's grace on planet Earth.

God started breaking his own rules long before redemption. Way back at Creation he thought up some pretty wild exceptions to what we would consider "the norm." God's oddball animals and plants give our planet a whimsical and unpredictable charm. And the human population, with its myriad differences, is not less filled with wonder. An eminent university psychologist insists that people should be as different from each other as possible so we will grow as individuals and as a society. Our differences make the world go 'round.

Most of us were taught rules as children: rules at the dining table, rules for play, rules for friendship, and so on. We started out believing life would be fair to us if we followed the rules. So we try to do well, to be "good." Then we, or someone we love, falls through the cracks. We experience some of life's exceptions, and we don't like it one bit. When things go wrong, we wonder, *Why? What about the rules?* And we exclaim, "This just isn't fair!"

It isn't fair, but then, God never said life would be fair. Life on this earth doesn't always play out according to rigid rules. Remember, God has been creating exceptions to the rules since time began. I, for one, am glad he doesn't treat me according to "the rules." Where would I be if I got what my sin really deserves?

We all need a way to survive our losses, to live with life's exceptions, to celebrate our joys in spite of our sorrows. We do that by grace, by remembering that God is never taken by surprise. His exceptions were built in before the dawn of time. So when you or the people you love fall through the cracks, you are going to fall right into his arms of grace. Hang in there! And learn to glory in the fact that God's grace in exceptions makes life fun as well as functional.

I gather grace-filled encouragement from readers all over the country in the form of inspirational quotes and jokes. I enjoy cutting them out and pasting them together on the pages of my newsletter, *The Love Line*. My readers are blessed, they send me more "grace notes" to share, and God's grace just increases, like compounding interest. "I am too blessed to be stressed," wrote one reader. Another said, "I enjoy the cherries, and spit the pits!" These people are exceptions to the way life beats us up. They choose to celebrate the gift of grace.

Friend, if your life is bumpy these days, follow my husband's example. Grab the grace to be real and to be as odd as you really are. Make pleasing designs with the bumps of life rather than trying to get rid of them. Think of Bill, and remember that grace is like peanut butter: you can't spread it around without getting some on yourself!

And God is able to make all grace abound to you,
so that in all things at all times, having all that
you need, you will abound in every good work.

2 CORINTHIANS 9:8

❦

Surprise!

PATSY CLAIRMONT

*Afflictions are often the black folds in which God
doth set the jewels of his children's graces,
to make them shine better.*

CHARLES SPURGEON

What a surprise that the Lord would lavish us with his favor!

I still become almost giddy at the thought that today I am an author. It makes me giggle to even write the word *author.* I had wanted to write ever since I was a child, but I took a sharp left turn out of the school's front door at age sixteen, when I quit school, and veered right into trouble.

After years of flailing about, I stepped onto God's narrow path and into his wide swath of grace. His path eventually led me into — surprise! — writing.

Another grace gift came to me packaged in blue. I'll never forget when I unwrapped the bundle of blankets tucked around my eldest son and found inside a miracle. I couldn't believe that God could bring forth good out of my damaged life, much less a black-haired, brown-eyed squirming wonder. For me, Marty's birth was a sign of God's favor, unmerited by me.

But it doesn't take a lot of living to discover that all of life's surprises aren't worthy of a party. The first smack of reality starts at birth with a firm whack (surprise!) across our backsides, which should prepare us for the jolts ahead. Yet life continues to catch us off guard with those moments that cause us to reel.

I'm telling you, life can be a blessing . . . and life can be brutal.

When I was thirteen, I was the pitcher for a neighborhood baseball game. I took a line drive (surprise!) right to my throat. Ah, but here's the good news: I threw the bum out at first base before I collapsed. So there!

I still can recall in living color another time when blood gushed from my knees after I catapulted myself into the air at an amazing speed, all because I attempted to stop my bicycle by squeezing both hand brakes hard. How was I to know (surprise!) that "easy" goes a long way? It was my maiden voyage.

My youngest son, Jason, will not forget the day Mom slammed the car door (surprise!) on his fingers. In my overstated way, I gave the door the old heave-ho and, much to my horror and his, smashed Jason's fingers. I was grateful no digits were broken, just a piece of my heart to think I could have brought pain to his little life.

In blessings we expect to find God's generous grace. Yet his grace is also extended to us in brutal moments. In fact, I have found that, like a diamond bracelet presented on a square of black velvet, some of the most exquisite presentations of this merciful attribute of God's are often in the dark hours of our soul.

When the batter hit me with that baseball, I wanted to hurt him. Well, at least his pride. I savored the umpire's cry of, "You're out!" But I'm grateful the Lord doesn't respond that way to me. For how many times have I hurt the Lord with my retaliatory attitude? My instant response may be to get even with the other guy, only then to experience God's willingness to embrace me despite my insolence.

My hubby and I are feisty folks and given to disputes. But the Lord has huddled with Les and me in our "time-outs" like a referee to help us become more gracious with each other.

Sometimes I've caused myself pain, but the Lord has picked up this scuffed maiden and set my feet back on solid ground. Sometimes I've felt bruised by my own expectations of others, and sometimes, in my rush, I've made poor judgment calls. And how often, in my negligence, have I, like a child going out to play, slammed my heart's door closed, only to have grace flood in a window?

Hmm, perhaps I've been wrong. Most events in our lives might well be worthy of calling up friends to join in a celebration. For, on careful scrutiny, we find that God's grace-filled fingerprints are all over our lives. Surprise!

> *The grace of our Lord was poured out*
> *on me abundantly.*
>
> 1 TIMOTHY 1:14

❧

Flowers for Erin

THELMA WELLS

✌

Grace is glory begun, and glory is but grace perfected.
JONATHAN EDWARDS

When I first met Sandy fifteen years ago, she was a good woman, but not a Christian. When she did receive Christ as her personal savior, she had no idea that on January 23, 1999, she would experience the kindness of her loving heavenly Father the way she did. In fact, she told me, had he not shown her his grace in a tangible way, she didn't think she would have made it.

Early on the morning of January 20, Sandy received a call from her son, Tom, asking her to pray for his baby girl who had just been born a few minutes after midnight. Though she was four weeks early, Erin was a big baby, but she had severe internal problems.

Sandy prayed steadily. Less than twenty-four hours later, she received another call from Tom telling her, through sobs, that Erin was not doing well, and if Sandy and her husband wanted to see her before she died, they needed to leave *now*. Sandy prayed and cried for most of the five-hour trip to Detroit.

When they arrived at the hospital, Sandy saw her precious little Erin hooked up to a maze of machines and tubes. The baby looked so helpless and vulnerable. Between visits, Sandy retreated to her Bible to search for words of comfort and some clue as to why all this was happening. She came upon Jeremiah 29:11–14:

> "For I know the plans I have for you," declares the LORD, "plans to prosper you and not to harm you, plans to give you hope and a future. Then you will call upon me and come and pray to me, and I will listen to you. You will seek me and find me when you seek me with all your heart. I will be found by you," declares the LORD, "and will bring you back from captivity. I will gather you from all the nations and places where I have banished you," declares the LORD, "and will bring you back to the place from which I carried you into exile."

Sandy was sure that God had just given her a clear message: Erin would recover and be fine. But this was not to be. Little Erin was welcomed into God's loving arms later that night.

Though Sandy felt the presence of the Lord in a very constant and comforting way, she shed many tears for *her* loss that night. While she knew she hadn't really "lost" Erin (for she truly knew where the baby was), she experienced nearly overwhelming grief.

The following day was a busy one, making funeral arrangements and buying flowers. Flowers are a very important part of Sandy's life; she loves to tend her flower beds with loving care. But when she went to the florist, Sandy could only mourn the many types of flowers that she would never get to plant with Erin. She could think only of all the things she would never get to do with her granddaughter.

She asked the florist to put together an arrangement of flowers that she had in her yard at home: lilies, agapanthus, daisies, delphiniums, coneflowers, Gerber daisies, and many more. She knew there was no way any florist in Detroit could find most of those flowers. After all, it was January!

On the day of the funeral, Sandy found herself in the church alone with Erin for a few minutes. As the funeral director carried in arrangement after arrangement of flowers, Sandy saw the one she had ordered. Every flower in her yard was in that basket! "What a powerful reminder of my Father's love for me," Sandy told me, "that he would provide the most perfect flowers for my baby granddaughter the only time I would be able to give them to her."

As Sandy continued to watch the parade of flowers, she began to mourn that Erin would never have a wedding; would never be a bride. At that very moment, the funeral director carried in a vase brimming with tall white flowers. Sandy walked over to those flowers and received a most powerful message that this was indeed Erin's bridal bouquet. Erin was now the bride of Christ!

As Sandy continued to feel great sorrow for her loss, she cried to God that her grandbaby would never go on dates or to dances; she would never get an orchid corsage from a boy. Through her tears Sandy looked at the flower arrangement again, and there, right in the center of the vase, was a stem of baby orchids. "I looked at the card on the arrangement," Sandy said, "only to find yet another hug from God. The flowers were from my two most special friends from my Bible study back home. No matter where I turned, no matter what direction my grief was taking, God was there so personally to prove to me that he knew what and how I was feeling, and *all* of the comfort he had to give was available for me in that moment. All I had to do was stop and listen."

On January 23, 1999, Sandy understood Jeremiah 29:11–14 in a new light. She saw the plans God had for her Erin. They were plans to give her a future, a future filled with beauty and happiness as his bride. "And the plans he has for me?" Sandy said. "I find bits and pieces of them daily, and I am constantly amazed at his originality in presenting them to me. When I have eyes to see, I receive endless gifts of grace to cherish and celebrate."

My friend, God's grace shows up in *all* our circumstances if we would but recognize it. When we experience grief and sorrow and things don't turn out the way we want them to, God has not left us. He gives us more and more grace when the burdens are greater and greater.

There are times in all of our lives when grief of some kind sweeps over our soul, and we find ourselves looking for answers and comfort. Isn't it wonderful to know that a loving God cares enough about what we're going through to reach down and stroke our brow, or hug us through the arms of other people, or kiss us with the sweetness of kind words. Or send us flowers. As my friend Barbara Johnson says, "God will wrap you in his comfort blanket." Let him hold you now.

Grace and peace be yours in abundance.
Praise be to the God . . . [who] has given us
new birth into a living hope . . . and into an
inheritance that can never perish, spoil or
fade. . . . In this you greatly rejoice, though

> *now for a little while you may have had to*
> *suffer grief in all kinds of trials. These have*
> *come so that your faith . . . may be proved*
> *genuine and may result in praise, glory and*
> *honor when Jesus Christ is revealed.*

1 Peter 1:2–7

&

Singing in the Rain

BARBARA JOHNSON

❧

Grace is the ability to let your light shine after your fuse is blown.

While flying to a conference recently, I was leafing through the airline's magazine which has items you can purchase through a catalog. I spied a darling ad showing a black umbrella. The description said, "Gray skies are gonna clear up!" The umbrella opened to reveal a blue sky with white fluffy clouds floating by. It was like moving out from under dismal rain clouds to a clear bright day at the touch of a button.

I had to order that umbrella, of course, because it was such an encouragement to me! When it arrived in the mail, it was even better than depicted in the advertisement. It brought inspiration and joy into my gloomy days.

None of us can avoid the gray skies and dreariness in life. At times we get absolutely drenched with troubles. But you know what? They're gonna clear up! Nothing lasts forever. The stuff we go through is only temporary. There will be lots of clearings along the way. And one day we will enjoy blue skies forever.

My new umbrella is in my Joy Room at home. I haven't had much of a chance to use it because in California our days are filled with so much sun and fun. But just like other people, I have my share of spiritual gray skies. When they come, I have to ask God to remind me that there is a clearing ahead. There is a bright shiny day coming. Soon enough, it will be time for a new beginning.

Each one of us needs a new beginning at some point or other. But it needn't come with a bang of fireworks or a streaking comet. New beginnings often come slowly. They may even sneak up on you — like a tiny ray of sun slipping out from beneath a black cloud. You can be inspired by the smallest things, so keep your eyes open.

Consider these: A tea kettle singing on the stove inspired the steam engine. An apple falling from a tree inspired the discovery of gravity. A shirt waving on a clothesline inspired the balloon. A spider web strung across a garden path inspired the suspension bridge. God will use the simplest realities to inspire something bigger and better in your life.

NBC news anchor John Chancellor once quipped, "You want to make God laugh, tell him your plans." God has much greater ambitions for us than we have for ourselves. He laughs at our paltry plans, then plots to surprise us with the greatness of his grace. Author C. S. Lewis referred to God's extravagant nature when he said, "You thought you were being made into a decent little cottage? God wants to make of your life a palace!" Of course, we have to learn to live with the rain and the fog while we're waiting for our skies to clear up and God's glory to be revealed. But rest your hope upon the grace that will crown your life when Jesus' plan unfolds. With the touch of a button he will draw you under the protection of his umbrella where you can enjoy sunny skies forever.

An optimist is someone who tells you to cheer up when things are going her way. I am more than an optimist. I have been ground in the mill, processed in the plant, and mashed like a potato. I am here to tell you that I am a firm believer in the Bible and its promises. I have learned that grace is not freedom from the storm, but peace within the storm.

So open your umbrella! Get out from under the downpour and remember the blue skies — they're on their way. In the meantime, by grace, you can celebrate the reality of God's extravagant plans for you and go on singing in the rain.

Set your hope fully on the grace to be given you
when Jesus Christ is revealed.

1 PETER 1:13

∾

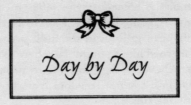

Day by Day

PATSY CLAIRMONT

❧

If God only made his presence known in
the momentous, how barren our lives would be of
grace-filled windows to the sacred.

DEBRA KLINGSPORN

I stood in the grocery store checkout lane and watched the cashier's fingers race over the number pads while the register tape spewed forth. For a moment, as the tape stretched out and then began to curl up, it reminded me of my life.

At this juncture I have tallied more days than I can believe. They seem to have raced along, and often there was a price I paid. Now when I'm asked my age I have to stop to figure it out (duh). I'm surprised to find that the accumulation of days is so hefty and that my children are established adults.

As I write it is March, the month of the lion and the lamb. I'm amazed because it seems as though New Year's Day was just last week. March. Hmm, that means nine weeks have passed, sixty-three days since the year began.

What did I spend those days on? Let's see ... I traveled to three states. I took time out for the flu and a sinus infection. I read a book, tried a few new recipes, attended a concert, and did some serious writing. I visited with friends, attended church, and ate out.

Interesting, isn't it, how quickly a day fills up and then spills over into another day, leaving us exhilarated, exhausted, or perhaps relieved. Before long, the days turn into months and the months into years. After a while we're left scratching our heads, wondering what we did with our time. Some memories of our bygone days have faded or blurred while others are like a hologram card, dimensional and detailed.

Not every day speeds through its allotted hours, of course. How well I remember thinking when I was in labor with each of my sons, "This day will never end!" Then followed the endless stacks of diapers to change and formula to mix, and I wondered if I would get through some of those ammonia-filled days of spit-up. Yet in no time at all I was packing away the baby clothes and unpacking the bank account to assist with their first cars. And when they left home for good, the dirty diapers weren't what remained paramount in my memory; rather, the nursery rhymes, the patty-cakes, and the lullabies were cradled in this mama's heart.

I love that a day has boundaries so I can measure it. From sunrise to sunset, from morning to evening, from a sunlit day to a starlit night, hours collect into a lifetime. As I reflect on my collection, I'm reminded what a gift life is and, therefore, how precious each twenty-four-hour increment is. I also realize that the days I thought would never end are some of the sweeter memories that I hold up now like a multi-faceted diamond refracting light.

One of those sparkling facets is God's extravagant grace, which has been so clearly extended to me throughout my life's journey. He helped me to take the next step on the good days and on the bad — especially the bad.

Dear friend, embrace your day — this day — it is a gift. Take the Lord's hand. He will help you to unwrap the day and then to celebrate it. And his grace will be sufficient for any need you have.

Whatever marches into your day, remember who is the Lion of Judah and the Lamb of God. He tallies our days and tends our nights. He who paid the ultimate price to give us life holds us safely in his eternal hands.

> *All the days ordained for me were written in*
> *your book before one of them came to be.*
>
> PSALM 139:16

∾

Conclusion: Indiglo

LUCI SWINDOLL

ﾷ

few days ago I was given a night-light called "Indiglo." I love night-lights. And this particular one is interesting because it's completely flat, small, oval, and a solid mass of iridescent blue. Even though it's a tiny little thing, it illumines my entire bathroom. From my bed I fall asleep watching the room bathe itself in blue light, feeling secure that the darkness won't cause me to stumble if I get up during the night. It's peace-producing.

My night-light brings back memories of lying in bed at night as a little girl. I remember cars turning the corner in front of our house, their headlights momentarily invading the darkness of my bedroom, against the door, then the wall, the ceiling, and ultimately my bed, in one long shaft of moving light. That light made me feel safe, as if God were in the yard, checking on me with his flashlight, just to let me know he was around and everything was okay.

Oh, and this: my favorite watch has a backlight. It's not a pretty thing, nor does it always match what I wear, but who cares? It gives me a good feeling to know that I can tell time anywhere I am — be it a theater, a tunnel, a dark street, a polar ice cap. (I've never been to the South Pole, but I'm ready should we start drifting.)

With the world living in so much emotional and spiritual darkness, you'd think everybody would gravitate toward light. But they don't. Often, people don't even know they're groping and fretting in the dark. They wander around without the peace, safety, and comfort that light brings.

In this book, my friends and I have told stories of how God is teaching us to unwrap, appreciate, enjoy, share, and celebrate the gifts of his grace. As we open our hearts to you, it is our hope that you will open your heart to him and see all the ways God is illuminating your path with grace. Right in your own household, backyard, neighborhood, workplace . . . there is grace in abundance.

When we live in the light we see it, recognize it for what it is, thank God for it, and eagerly pass it on to somebody else. Jesus told us he is the light of the world, and whoever follows him will never walk in darkness, but will have the light of life. What a gift—that we will not only walk in light but we will reflect his light.

We encourage you to be "indiglo." Each one of us— Barbara, Sheila, Marilyn, Thelma, Patsy, and I—wants you to shine where you are. It's possible, because everyone who follows Jesus has his light.

Five hundred years before the birth of Christ, the Greek poet Pindar wrote these insightful words:

> We are things of a day.
> What are we?
> What are we not?
> The shadow of a dream is man, no more.
> But when the brightness comes, and God gives it,
> there is a shining of light on men,
> and their life is sweet.

I've felt that brightness. I've experienced its warmth and glow. I know how it feels to have it shine on me. It's extravagant grace.

Pindar was right: when it's shining, life is sweet.

Faith

EXTRAVAGANT
2003 Grace

Women of

Sacramento, CA	February 21-22
Memphis, TN	March 14-15
Columbus, OH	March 28-29
Kansas City, MO	April 4-5
Shreveport, LA	May 2-3
Louisville, KY	May 16-17
Billings, MT	May 30-31
Anaheim, CA	June 6-7
Charleston, SC	June 13-14
Ft. Lauderdale, FL	June 20-21
Washington, DC	June 27-28
Dallas, TX	July 11-12
Toronto, ON	July 18-19
Denver, CO	July 25-26
Atlanta, GA	August 1-2
Oklahoma City, OK	August 8-9
Ames, IA	August 15-16
Chicago, IL	August 22-23
Anaheim, CA	September 5-6
St. Paul, MN	September 12-13
Albany, NY	September 19-20
Detroit, MI	September 26-27
Hartford, CT	October 3-4
Portland, OR	October 10-11
Vancouver, B.C.	October 17-18
Charlotte, NC	October 24-25
Omaha, NE	October 31-November 1
Philadelphia, PA	November 7-8
Orlando, FL	November 14-15

**This schedule is subject to change
Please call 1-800-247-1899

Extravagant Grace

IS BASED ON THE POPULAR
WOMEN OF FAITH CONFERENCE.

Women of Faith partners with various
Christian organizations, including
Campus Crusade for Christ International,
Crossings Book Club,
Integrity Music, International Bible Society
Partnerships, Inc., and World Vision
to provide spiritual resources for women.

**For more information about Women of Faith
or to register for one of our nationwide
conferences, call 1-800-49-FAITH.**

www.womenoffaith.com

Resources for Women of Faith℠

BOOKS/AUDIO

WOMEN OF FAITH BIBLE STUDY SERIES

WOMEN OF FAITH WOMEN OF THE BIBLE STUDY SERIES

WOMEN OF FAITH Zondervan*Groupware*™

Inspirio's innovative and elegant gift books capture the joy and encouragement that is an integral part of the Women of Faith[SM] movement.

Joy for a Woman's Soul
Promises to Refresh Your Spirit
ISBN: 0-310-97717-7

Grace for a Woman's Soul
Reflections to Renew Your Spirit
ISBN: 0-310-97996-X

Simple Gifts
Unwrapping the Special Moments of Everyday Life
ISBN: 0-310-97811-4

Padded Hardcover
4 x 7
208 pages

Verses from the New International Version of the Bible have been collected into this volume to inspire Women of Faith[SM] on their spiritual journey.

Prayers for a Woman of Faith[SM]
ISBN: 0-310-97336-8

Hardcover
5-1/4 x 5-1/4
128 pages

We want to hear from you.
Please send your comments about this book to us
in care of zreview@zondervan.com. Thank you.

GRAND RAPIDS, MICHIGAN 49530 USA

WWW.ZONDERVAN.COM